"I'm by nature a loner . . . until I couldn't do it any longer. Wish I had read this book when Jesus forced me into relationships. I would have had less wounds or, at least, would have understood the wounds, how I got them, gave them to others, and where I (and they) could go for healing. What a wonderful and helpful book! It will make a major difference in your life and the lives of everybody you love. Read this book and you will want to be my friend for recommending it to you."

Steve Brown, Author; professor at Reformed Seminary, Orlando; teacher for the national radio program, Key Life

"Relationships are messy . . . but they don't have to remain that way. In their new book, *Relationships: A Mess Worth Making*, Lane and Tripp provide us with invaluable help for unraveling the complexities of relating to others. Avoiding trite and complicated techniques so common in other books, these gifted authors remind us that transforming our own hearts is the key to transforming our relationships."

Robert Jeffress, Pastor; author of *Second Chance, Second Act*

"Apart from loving God with all our heart, soul, mind, and strength, nothing matters more to God than how we love one another. So many of us settle for too little—for superficial, safe relationships in our marriages, our families and our churches. I am so glad that Paul and Tim have written a book to guide us into deeper, richer relationships. I pray we'll have the courage to follow their counsel."

Bob Lepine, Cohost, FamilyLife Today

"Paul Tripp and Timothy Lane are right: Relationships are messy! But in their new book, Paul and Tim show readers how to clean up their old and neglected relationships to where they sparkle and shine like new. *Relationships: A Mess Worth Making* is perfect For anyone who's ever had a mother, a Father, a husband, a wife, a friend, a neighbor, a dog, a cot . . . ."

Doug Herman, Author of *Time for a Pure Revolution*; Founder of Pure Revolution Conferences & Resources

RELATIONSHIPS

A Mess Worth Making

Timothy S. Lane and Paul David Tripp

www.newgrowthpress.com

New Growth Press, Greensboro 27404

© 2006, 2008 by Timothy S. Lane and Paul David Tripp
All rights reserved. Published 2008

Cover Design: Matt Nowicki
Typesetting: Robin Black, www.blackbirdcreative.biz

ISBN-10: 0-9770807-6-5
ISBN-13: 978-0-9770807-6-2

Library of Congress Cataloging-in-Publication Data
Lane, Timothy S.
Relationships : a mess worth making / Timothy S. Lane and Paul David Tripp.
p. cm.
Includes bibliographical references and index.
ISBN 978-0-9770807-6-2
1. Interpersonal relations—Religious aspects—Christianity. I. Tripp, Paul David, 1950- II. Title.
BV4597.52.L36 2008
248.4—dc22

                                        2008015198

Printed in the United States of America

27 26 25 24 23 22 21 20   17 18 19 20 21

To our wives,

Barbara and Luella

Contents

Acknowledgments

When someone writes a book, the reader's assumption is that the author is an expert on the subject. Let us say unequivocally that our readers should not make that assumption about us! This is especially true when one writes on relationships. There is nothing more complex and challenging in life. In the first chapter, we talk about our own struggle to love others well, including each other. We first wrote that section as a brief introduction. But upon reflection, we thought it should be in the body of the book. We did not want people to forget that we too are sinners, daily dependent on God's grace to do what we encourage others to do.

Yet the acknowledgment of struggle and failure should not overshadow the hopeful truth that in Christ relationships can be maintained and repaired. They can flourish! They can become deeper and more meaningful than they were before they were ruptured by sin. We hope that both aspects of relationships come through in this book. Relationships are messy; they are also what God uses to rescue us from ourselves. Through them, God shows us our inability to love others without first finding our strength in our relationship with the God who created and redeemed us.

In light of this, we want to thank the people who have taught us the most about our need for God's grace. First, thanks to the families in which we grew up, our parents and siblings who have taught us so much. Second, thanks to our wives and children, who continue to watch us struggle and grow as husbands and fathers. Third, we are grateful to the churches and ministries we have served; they have helped us apply what we write about. Fourth, we thank the staff and faculty of CCEF, who have challenged us and encouraged us along the way. And finally, thanks to the churches where we are currently involved. Growth in grace is certainly a community project!

Once again, we are very grateful for the editorial work of Sue Lutz and her staff. This book has been much improved by her keen oversight and skill. The editing process itself has been a place to grow in our relationships with one another. For that, we can all be thankful.

As you read this book, we hope you will see that we don't need new or sophisticated techniques to see relationships flourish. It all boils down to basic character qualities that can only be formed in the heart by the gospel. This is how relationships grow and communities form to reflect God's glory and grace. We hope this book will move you down that path in significant ways. Writing it has done that for us.

Timothy S. Lane and Paul David Tripp
June 5, 2006

1

The Shortest and Most Important
Chapter of This Book

Writing a book is always a journey of unexpected turns. Try as you may to chart your course, you never wind up exactly where you've planned. This chapter is one of those unexpected turns. As we finished writing this book, we realized that we should explain to you how it was written. What you are about to read is a book on relationship that was written *in* relationship. When we coauthored *How People Change*, we divided up the chapters and wrote separately. However, we decided to write this book together. We worked at Tim's house—Tim at the computer and Paul pacing back and forth across the room. We discussed our way through sentences, paragraphs, pages, and chapters. When we finished, we both agreed that this process was one of the most unique and enjoyable ministry experiences of our lives.

What resulted from our collaboration is not just an examination, but an actual example of broken people in broken community experiencing the reconciling grace of God. We have written as flawed people in close relationship who have experienced God's grace in daily life and ministry. We have not written out of the wisdom of success, but out of the wisdom of striving. A brief history of our relationship will illustrate this point.

About five years ago, Paul was working at the Christian Counseling & Educational Foundation leading the department for local church-based training. The faculty of CCEF came to see that this job was too big for one person and decided to hire a seasoned pastor to partner with Paul. It was decided that Tim was just the kind of man to fill this role. The two of us began our work with excitement and mutual appreciation. However, problems arose when we, as two leaders who had known each other only from a safe distance, began working together in the same room! It became apparent that, although we shared a vision, we had very different personalities and gifts. It didn't take long for sin, weakness, and failure to rear their ugly heads. Minor offenses and major misunderstandings began to get in the way of our mutual appreciation—and the work God had brought us together to do.

This was a crucial moment. Would we give in to disillusionment and discouragement, or would we commit ourselves to do what we regularly teach others to do? We decided that our only choice was to trust Christ the way we ask others to, and give him an opportunity to work *in* us so that he could work *through* us.

We are quick to say that we are not heroes of relationship. In fact, the opposite is true. Our aim is that this book will help you look through the shattered glass of our sin to see the glory of a Redeemer who is ever-present, always at work to rescue and change us. We want you to know that the men who wrote this book are just like you in both struggle and potential. We are sinners with the capacity to do great damage to ourselves and our relationships. We need God's grace to save us from ourselves. But we are also God's children, which means that we have great hope and potential—not hope that rests on our gifts, experience, or track record, but hope that rests in Christ. Because he is in us and we are in him, it is right to say that our potential *is* Christ!

We are well aware that we are smack-dab in the middle of God's process of sanctification. And because this is true, we will struggle again. Selfishness, pride, an unforgiving spirit, irritation, and impatience will certainly return. But we are neither afraid nor hopeless. We have experienced what God can do in the middle of the mess. This side of heaven, relationships and ministry are always shaped in the forge of struggle. None of us get to relate to perfect people or avoid the effects of the fall on the work we attempt to do. Yet, amid the mess, we find the highest joys of relationship and ministry.

We want to affirm to you that what you will find in this book is true. We know it is true not only because we have examined the book's theology and found it to be orthodox, but also because we have tested the book's God and found him to be faithful again and again. What the book has to offer is not the wisdom of two men who have arrived, but the worship of two needy men who want to point you to the unfathomable and accessible resources of the God who has been with us and is with you. He is near, with, and in you. This means there is hope for you, even in relationships that leave you confused and disappointed.

May you experience his grace daily, as we do.

2

Why Bother?

My God, my God, why have you forsaken me?
Why are you so far from saving me,
so far from the words of my groaning?
O my God, I cry out by day, but you do not answer,
by night, and am not silent.

Psalm 22:1–2

"I had such high hopes for our friendship. What went wrong? I thought I had finally found someone I could trust."

"I can't believe you are questioning my integrity after all the things I have done for you. It's not like I am the only one who has failed in this relationship. You've hurt me, too."

"You see, this is what you always do. I come to you and you turn the table on me. You are so good at making other people feel guilty for your failures! The problem with you is that you are much better at recognizing other people's faults than you are your own. You don't have a clue how much you have hurt me. You betrayed our trust when you told them what I said."

"You never told me I couldn't say anything about what you shared with me. I didn't know you would be so sensitive about it."

"I thought you cared enough for me that I wouldn't have to tell you not to talk to someone else! I thought our relationship was as important to you as it is to me."

"You see, that's the problem. You always act like you are more committed to this relationship than I am. So you watch me like a hawk, just waiting to pounce on any hint of failure."

"Why does it always go here? We can't even have a discussion about the weather without it ending in accusation."

Sound Familiar?

As you eavesdropped on this conversation, did it sound familiar? You may not have used the same words, but you have probably felt the same way at some time in your life. These words may remind you of a specific relationship and a particular person. You've felt the sting of hurt and disappointment. You know that you have disappointed others too. It is clear to you that no relationship ever delivers what you dreamt it could. Your fantasy collides with reality, and reality bites!

"I can't believe you would do such a thing for me! It is so encouraging that I did not have to go through this alone."

"I've gotten as much as I have given. Your friendship has been a constant source of encouragement."

"Yeah. You know, when we first met, neither one of us had any idea what God would do through our friendship."

"What I appreciate is that while it hasn't always been easy, you have been committed to dealing with our problems and disagreements in a constructive way. Your honesty is refreshing."

"And you've modeled patience and a willingness to listen, even when it was hard. God has used you in my life to help me speak honestly, but in a more godly manner."

"I suspect it won't always be this comfortable, but it is encouraging that we are committed to dealing with our future problems this way."

Familiar Words?

You may not have used these exact words either, but we hope you can identify with this experience of mutual friendship and encouragement. God has put people in your life and placed you in theirs. When you look back, you can see their imprint on your character. There have been times when you were very glad not to go through life alone. You have been greeted by patience and grace, even after a failure. And you too have been willing to forgive and have experienced the blessing of doing so.

Two Worlds

Elise was so thankful for the circle of friends God had given her. The first couple of months had been extremely lonely after she moved out of state to take a new job. Before moving she had never imagined how much she would miss her church and friends. The one thing that kept her going was Kurt's commitment to follow her, so they could continue their relationship and get married in the not-too-distant future.

It wasn't long before Elise began to connect with people at a good church. She had become particularly close to Amanda and Marta. She was thankful that God had brought them into her life. Things seemed like they were going well: she had friends nearby and Kurt would be with her soon.

Then things began to change. First, Kurt's daily text messages weren't daily anymore. Then the weekly emails stopped arriving. Elise began to panic when she waited for the Friday night phone call (the highlight of her week) and it never came. She called Kurt on Saturday to ask him if everything was okay. He said he was fine, but he clearly wasn't. The next week was marked by even less contact—just a couple of short text messages. Then on Monday a lengthy email came, but not the one Elise wanted. Kurt wrote that he had reconsidered. He wasn't going to move to where she was, and he thought they should just "move on." Elise was crushed. Not only had Kurt ended their relationship, but he had done it by email!

For the next several days, Elise tried to surround herself with friends since all she did was cry when she was alone. Their love and support kept her going. On one side, Amanda and Marta had been unbelievably kind and understanding. But on the other, Kurt had left her feeling betrayed. She didn't think she would ever get over it. She wondered whether relationships were worth the risk of this kind of pain.

We all live in these two worlds in some way. Some of our deepest joys and most painful hurts have been in relationships. There are times we wish we could live alone and other times we are glad we don't. What is certain is that we all have been shaped significantly by relationships that are full of both sorrow and joy.

Take a moment to reflect on the relationships in your life. Think about the relationships in your family while you were growing up. What were the unspoken rules your family followed? How did you handle conflict? What was the typical method for solving problems? Were there regular patterns of forgiveness? Did you ever see forgiveness sought and granted? What were the normal ways you communicated? Who typically had the floor? Did you grow up in a quiet or loud family? What was conversation like around the dinner table? Were there certain taboo subjects or was everything fair game? How was anger expressed? Was it handled in a positive way? In the busyness of family life, how much investment was made in keeping relationships healthy? Were people motivated positively or with threats and guilt? Was your home a place to relax, or did you feel like you were walking on eggshells? To what degree was serving one another modeled and encouraged within the family? What kind of relationship did your family have with the surrounding community?

Your answers to these basic questions can show you how your family shaped your views on relating to others. Have the values of your family become your values? Have the struggles of your family become your struggles? Our family of origin is just one of many influences on our view of relationships. You have not become who you are all by yourself, which is why relationships are so important. They are inescapable and powerfully influential. The difficulty is that sin and grace coexist in all of them. Sin gets in the way of what grace can do, while grace covers what sin causes. Our relationships vividly display this dynamic mixture of gold and dross.

Oh No! Not Another Book on Relationships!

Since your local bookstores are already crammed with books and magazines about relationships, why take the time to read this one? What can we offer that would interest both the most naïve and most jaded people? We want to highlight the unique lens God gives his children to look at their lives. This lens will help you make your way through the intersection of sin and grace in relationships. Without it, you will remain naïve or grow cynical. When you face problems, you will be left only with human wisdom and techniques that produce short-term solutions, but can't promise lasting personal and interpersonal change. The fatal flaw of human wisdom is that it promises that you can change your relationships without needing to change *yourself* When that perspective rules, you end up settling for far less than what

God desires for your life and your friendships. As Christian author C. S. Lewis observed,

> Our Lord finds our desires not too strong, but too weak. We are half-hearted creatures, fooling about with drink and sex and ambition when infinite joy is offered us, like an ignorant child who wants to go on making mud pies in a slum because he cannot imagine what is meant by the offer of a holiday at the sea. We are far too easily pleased.[1]

In our human wisdom, we would settle for relational détente, but God wants to bring us to the end of ourselves so that we would see our need for a relationship with him as well as with others. Every painful thing we experience in relationships is meant to remind us of our need for him. And every good thing we experience is meant to be a metaphor of what we can only find in him. To quote C. S. Lewis again, this primary vertical relationship is foundational to everything the Bible says about relationships.

> When I have learnt to love God better than my earthly dearest, I shall love my earthly dearest better than I do now. In so far as I learn to love my earthly dearest at the expense of God and *instead* of God, I shall be moving towards the state in which I shall not love my earthly dearest at all. When first things are put first, second things are not suppressed but increased.[2]

It's probably clear that what Lewis is describing is not always evident in your life. It's not always evident in ours either. There are many indicators that reveal our tendency to reverse the order of things and put second things first. This is why we struggle with:

- Letting go of a moment of hurt
- Getting angry at the way our teenagers complicate our lives
- Becoming defensive when challenged
- Avoiding conflict out of fear

---

1   C. S. Lewis, *The Weight of Glory and Other Addresses* (New York: Harcourt Brace Jovanovich, 1960), 3–4.

2   C. S. Lewis, *Letters of C. S. Lewis* (New York: Harcourt Brace Jovanovich, 1966), 248.

- Being too political at work
- Being resigned to broken relationships that could be healed
- Gossiping about people
- Lying out of fear of what others will think
- Compromising our convictions to win others' approval
- Pursuing comfortable relationships and avoiding difficult ones
- Doubting God when our relationships are messy
- Envying other people's friendships
- Controlling relationships out of a desire for security
- Blowing up at people when our agendas are trampled
- Living in bitter isolation in the face of disappointment

That is why the topic of this book is so important. All of us need a clearer sense of what it means to put first things first and how Jesus enables us to do that. We also need to understand what practical changes are needed to create a new agenda for our relationships and what concrete steps we need to take as we seek to please God.

A Biblical Lens on Relationships

Because this topic is so comprehensive and has been written on extensively, we want to start with eight biblical facts that summarize the way God wants us to think about our relationships. These facts will shape the way we approach everything in this book. They won't be specifically discussed in every chapter, but they are the foundation for our model of healthy, godly relationships.

You were made for relationships

This fact takes us back to the beginning. It asks the basic questions, "Who are we, and how important are our relationships?" In Genesis 2:18, God says that it is not good for man to be "alone." This statement has more to do with God's design for humanity than Adam's neediness. God created us to be relational beings because he is a social God. God lives in community within the Trinity as Father, Son, and Spirit, and he made humanity in his image. Genesis 2 is not speaking primarily to Adam's experience of being lonely as much as it is revealing his nature as the person God created him to be. Because God created a communal being—someone designed for relationships—creation is incomplete without a suitable companion. While Genesis 2 does address how male and female complement each other, the implications are broader to include all human relationships. In addition, the word *helper*, used here for Eve, speaks throughout Scripture of the complementary nature of all human relationships. *Helper* is used primarily to describe a companion, not a fellow laborer.

The reason we know this is true is because the word *helper* is often used to describe God's relationship with his people. When used this way, it does not refer to God as our coworker or employee, but as our ultimate companion who brings things to the relationship that we could not bring ourselves (Psalms 27:9; 33:20–22). So God is not addressing Adam's workload, but rather the fact that he is a social being who lacks a suitable companion. Just as human beings were created with a vertical need for God's companionship, they are also created for the horizontal companionship of other people.

Genesis 2 points to the fact that relationships are a core component of who God has designed you to be. Relationship is so important to God that he brings his creative work to a climax by creating Eve. Together she and Adam can experience community—vertical and horizontal—in the presence of the living God.

In some way, all relationships are difficult

While the first fact is exciting, we still have to deal with reality. All of our relationships are less than perfect. They require work if they are going to thrive. Quickly on the euphoric heels of Genesis 2 comes Genesis 3, where the entrance of sin brings frustration and confusion into relationships. In Genesis 3, man and woman engage in accusation and slander. Genesis 4 gets even worse, with a man murdering his own brother.

While many of us have not committed murder, we still live on the continuum between murder, accusation, and blame. No wonder our relationships are so messy! Our struggle with sin is constantly revealed in them. If you want to enjoy any progress or blessing in your relationships, it will require you to admit your sin humbly and commit yourself to the work they require.

Each of us is tempted to make relationships the end rather than the means

When we reflect on Genesis 1–3, it becomes clear that the primary relationship Adam and Eve were intended to enjoy was their relationship with God. This vertical communion with God would provide the foundation for the horizontal community they were to have with each other. Everything God made pointed Adam and Eve to the primacy of their relationship with him. All of creation was to function as an arrow pointing to God. But in our sin we tend to treat people and creation as more important. The very things God created to reveal his glory become instead the glory we desire. This is where we see, with C. S. Lewis, that our desires are too weak, not too strong. We settle for the satisfaction of human relationships when they were meant to point us to the perfect relational satisfaction found only with God. The irony is that when we reverse the order and elevate creation above Creator, we destroy the relationships God intended—and would have enabled—us to enjoy.

There are no secrets that guarantee problem-free relationships

We all look for strategies or techniques that will free us from the pain of relationships and the hard work good relationships demand. We hope that better planning, more effective communication, clear role definitions, conflict resolution strategies, gender studies, and personality typing—to name just a few—will make the difference. There may be value in these things, but if they were all we needed, Jesus's life, death, and resurrection would be unnecessary or, at best, redundant.

Skills and techniques appeal to us because they promise that relational problems can be fixed by tweaking our behavior without altering the bent of our hearts. But the Bible says something very different. It says that Christ is the only real hope for relationships because only he can dig deep enough to address the core motivations and desires of our hearts.

At some point you will wonder whether relationships are worth it

At some point each of us will become discouraged and disappointed with a relationship. The health and maturity of a relationship are not measured by an absence of problems, but by the way the inevitable problems are handled. From birth to death, we are sinners living with other sinners. A good relationship involves honestly identifying the sin patterns that tend to trouble it. It also involves being humble and willing to guard yourself and the other person from these sin patterns. Because human conflict is the result of the spiritual battles in our hearts, wise relationships always seek to be aware of that deeper struggle. Even in times of peace, you must be vigilant regarding the way your relationships can be hijacked by the underlying desires of your hearts, which are subtly and constantly shifting.

How do you deal with relational disappointments? Do you blame, deny, run away, avoid, threaten, and manipulate? Or do you speak the truth, exhibit patience, approach people gently, ask for and grant forgiveness, overlook minor offenses, encourage and honor others? Let's admit that these questions touch us where we live from day to day. True Christian maturity does not get any more practical and concrete!

God keeps us in messy relationships for his redemptive purpose

This sixth fact reminds us that the very thing we would naturally seek to avoid is what God has chosen to use to make us more like him! Have you ever wondered why God doesn't just make your relationships better overnight? We often think that if God really cared for us, he would make our relationships easier. In reality, a difficult relationship is a mark of his love and care. We would prefer that God would just change the relationship, but he won't be content until the relationship changes us too. This is how God created relationships to function.

What happens in the messiness of relationships is that our hearts are revealed, our weaknesses are exposed, and we start coming to the end of ourselves. Only when this happens do we reach out for the help God alone can provide. Weak and needy people finding their hope in Christ's grace are what mark a mature relationship. The most dangerous aspect of your relationships is not your weakness, but your delusions of strength. Self-reliance is almost always a component of a bad relationship. While we would like to avoid the mess and enjoy deep and intimate community, God says that it is in the very process of working through the mess that intimacy is found. Which relationships are most meaningful to you? Most likely they are the ones that involved working through difficulty and hardship.

The fact that our relationships work as well as they do is a sure sign of grace

One of the biggest impediments we face in relationships is our spiritual blindness. We frequently do not see our sin, nor do we see the many ways in which God protects us and others from it. God constantly protects us from ourselves by restraining our sin. We are a lot like Elisha's servant in 2 Kings 6:15–22. He was overwhelmed by the enemy army that surrounded him until God opened his eyes to see the far more formidable army of angels God had sent to protect him. Why was it the servant could see only the enemies surrounding Israel, but not "the hills full of horses and chariots of fire" from the Lord? It was the spiritual blindness of unbelief.

How do you measure your potential in relationships? Do you measure the size of the problems or the magnitude of God's presence in your midst? Considering our sin, it is amazing that people get along at all! Each night the evening news begins with a litany of murders, rapes, and robberies that suggests that our communities are very dangerous places. Yet it often fails to cite the thousands of good things people do to make those same communities livable. Our view of our relationships can be just as slanted. We tend to see sins, weaknesses, and failures, rather than the good things God is accomplishing. If you look for God in your relationships, you will always find things to be thankful for.

Scripture offers a clear hope for our relationships

Does the challenge and mess of relationships leave you discouraged? Does the biblical honesty about human community shock you? Are you feeling overwhelmed by the hard work relationships require? If so, you are ready for this last fact: The shattered relationship between Father, Son, and Holy Spirit at the cross provides the basis for our reconciliation. No other relationship ever suffered more than what Father, Son, and Holy Spirit endured when Jesus hung on the cross and cried, "My God, my God, why have you forsaken me?" (Matthew

27:46). Jesus was willing to be the rejected Son so that our families would know reconciliation. Jesus was willing to become the forsaken friend so that we could have loving friendships. Jesus was willing to be the rejected Lord so that we could live in loving submission to one another. Jesus was willing to be the forsaken brother so that we could have godly relationships. Jesus was willing to be the crucified King so that our communities would experience peace.

In his life, death, and resurrection, Jesus brought reconciliation in two fundamental ways. Jesus reconciled us to God, which then becomes the foundation for the way he reconciles us to one another. As C. S. Lewis said, Christ restores first things so that second things are not suppressed but increased! When God reigns in our hearts, peace reigns in our relationships.

This work will only be complete in heaven, but there is much we can enjoy now. The New Testament offers hope that our relationships can be characterized by things like humility, gentleness, patience, edifying honesty, peace, forgiveness, compassion, and love. Isn't it wonderful that God's grace can make this possible, even for sinners in a fallen world! This hope challenges whatever complacency and discouragement we might have about our relationships because there is always more growth, peace, and blessing that God's grace can bring, even here on earth. The hope of the gospel invites us to a holy dissatisfaction with all of our relationships, even—especially—those with few major problems.

Our Goal and Hope

As you read this book, please keep in mind that our goal is to be as honest as the Bible is about relationships. If we succeed, this book will map onto your experience. In addition to being honest, we hope to be as positive as the gospel is about the potential of relationships. This will give you the encouragement you need to tackle the rewarding but difficult work of redemptive relationships. If you wonder, *Why bother?*, the answer is, "Because God did."

3

No Options

The man and his wife were both naked,
and they felt no shame.
Genesis 2:25

We had just moved to a new home and we were far from being settled. Life on every side seemed complicated and chaotic. Our schedule seemed ridiculously demanding. Our children ranged in ages from two to eleven, and they all seemed out of sorts. The weeks went by so fast, it seemed like I started putting on my trousers on Monday and it was Saturday before I got them zipped up!

Sure, we had family worship every morning and a fairly relaxed family dinner in the evening. We were dedicated to doing things as a family, but it all just seemed like a stressed-filled blur of duty. My wife and I tried to spend time together as a couple, but we hardly communicated any enthusiasm for our relationship. We were exhausted and had allowed irritation and impatience to come between us.

I had been elected to do a late-night run to the grocery store because, once again, we had little to put in the children's lunches for school the next day. I finished shopping and was waiting for the light to turn green so I could make my way home, when I began to think what it would be like to be single! I'm serious. I was completely overwhelmed and discouraged with the most important relationships in my life, and I wondered how I could successfully deal with what was on my plate.

The minute the thought crossed my mind, I was horrified! I love my children and I am privileged to know and be loved by my wife. I wouldn't want to live a second without them. But at that moment those relationships seemed so difficult and demanding. I loved my family, but that night in the car I hit the wall of the reality of relationships in a fallen world.

Everyone has hit that wall called, "Why bother with other people?" We reach points in our relationships where we wonder if they are worth it. A wife decides it's not worth opening up to her husband anymore. An employee goes to work, shuts his door, and only comes out when it is time to go home. A teenager comes home from school and goes to his room until he is cajoled to join the family for dinner. Someone probably dropped out of a small group this week because she didn't think it was worth the hassle. Family gatherings are reduced to people sharing the same geographical space, devoid of any meaningful relationship. The church meeting becomes a formality with little or no attempt to share in the lives of others. Neighbors live side by side for years, but no one knows anything significant about the other.

What do all of these people and scenarios have in common? They have all faced the difficulty of having relationships with flawed people in a broken world, and they have opted to check out. Is this a valid response? Is it okay to keep to ourselves so that we don't get hurt and don't hurt anyone else? What's wrong with playing it safe?

Yet something keeps dragging us back to other people. We know we are less than human when we are all alone. Why does the employee who works in isolation wonder what others are doing outside his office? Why is the teenager jealous when he sees his parents pay attention to his brother or sister when *he* made the decision to shut them out? Why does the person who chose to live apart from others describe his experience in terms of "loneliness"?

We live with this tension between self-protective isolation and the dream for meaningful relationships. Where are you on the continuum right now? Are you moving away from others because of a recent hurt? Are you moving toward others because you have been alone too long? What tendency do you observe in your life? Do you typically move in the direction of isolation or immersion? Do you tend toward independence or codependence? Every relational decision we make is moving in one of these directions. We are tempted to make a relationship either less or more than it was intended to be. Without a biblical model to explain the place relationships should have in your life, you will likely experience imbalance, confusion, conflicting desires, and general frustration. You just don't know how to navigate the minefield. Even the best relationships can surprise you with the challenges they present.

Two Extremes

While most of us don't tend to live at either of these extremes, we do move in the direction of isolation or immersion in all our relationships:

"I want to be safe."   "I need you in order to live."
(Isolation)   ◄──────►   (Immersion)

Figure 3-1

Where we are on the continuum varies with each relationship, but for most of us, our problems tend to cluster on one end of the continuum or the other. In most cases, whatever problems we have in relationships tend to fit one of three relational profiles.

The frustrated relationship

Here one person moves toward isolation while the other moves toward immersion. One dreams of being safe; the other dreams of being close and intimate. Imagine how differently these two would prepare for a vacation. The person seeking isolation is packing a stack of books, while the person seeking immersion is filling the schedule with activities to do together! How does it feel to live in this type of relationship? The isolationist feels smothered; the immersionist feels rejected. Since both of them regularly have their expectations frustrated, the relationship is perpetually disappointing. Each person thinks his perspective and expectations are fair and reasonable, so the shared disappointment eventually leads to anger.

The enmeshed relationship

Here both people move toward immersion. They ride the roller coaster of each other's emotions. Because they are so dependent on each other, they can be easily hurt when the other does not meet their needs. Because their expectations for the relationship are so high, they tend to live in isolation from other people. If these two were to take a vacation, they would spend every waking moment together. While you might think that similar expectations would lead to peace and harmony, it actually produces more problems—at least in this kind of relationship. Because each is looking to the other to satisfy very high relational expectations, they both become highly sensitive, easily hurt, and critical. Much of the energy in the relationship is spent dealing with minor offenses, real or perceived. Each feels hurt because his or her expectations of the other person are never completely fulfilled. They feel discouraged too because, no matter how hard they try, they never seem to measure up to the other's expectations. This kind of relationship is exhausting because the work required makes peace impossible.

The isolated relationship

Here both people move toward isolation. Each person is very aware of the dangers of relationships and constantly opts for safety.

Conversations are limited, safe, and impersonal. They tend to stay away from self-disclosure. The ideal vacation for these two would involve lots of time alone with minimal interaction. Each would read a different book, immersed in his or her own private world. This kind of relationship is complicated because the desire for safety and independence collides with the longing for relationship. Because they are communal beings made in God's image, both people long for some form of connection, no matter how small it may be. And although they both want safety, their desire for it separates them, making the relationship empty and disappointing.

In each scenario there is a relational impasse. In the frustrated relationship, the movement is away from the other. In the enmeshed relationship, the move toward the other is so extreme that it is impossible to satisfy expectations. In the isolated relationship, the movement towards safety precludes real relationship.

Do you recognize yourself in any of these profiles? Though all relationships are unique, you probably see qualities that characterize your relationships to some degree. (You can probably also think of relationships between other people that fit one or more of these descriptions.) The interesting point about each profile is that each is an unbalanced relationship because each person tends to make too much or too little of the relationship. Isolationists conclude that relationships are too difficult; they are not necessary and the effort is not worth it. ("I don't need relationships to be me.") On the other hand, immersionists are convinced that relationships are everything. ("Without relationships, I am nobody.") These conclusions are rooted in people's hearts and expectations. When things go wrong in relationships, the problem often starts there. So while relationships are not inherently dangerous, the expectations we bring to them can be. This is why it is important to ask questions about what God intended for this area of our lives. We need to ask, "What purpose does God intend relationships to serve in my life? As a person created in his image, what should my relationships look like?"

Our Communal God

All books on relationships raise the same questions we have asked so far. Unfortunately, however, most go on to answer these questions only from a horizontal perspective. But if it is true that people are made in the image of God, the first thing we need to do when we talk about relationships is to ask vertical questions. You will gain a greater understanding of the purpose of relationships not by examining humans, but by looking to God. Miroslav Volf begins with God to come to a conclusion about the essence of being human.

> Because the Christian God is not a lonely God, but rather a communion of the three persons, faith leads human beings into the divine *communio*. One cannot, however, have a self-enclosed communion with the Triune God—a "foursome," as it were—for the Christian God is not a private deity. Communion with this God is at once also communion with those others who have entrusted themselves in faith to the same God. Hence one and the same act of faith places a person into a new relationship both with God and with all others who stand in communion with God.[1]

---

1   Miroslav Volf, *After Our Likeness: The Church as the Image of the Trinity* (Grand Rapids: Eerdmans, 1998), 173.

Does this seem impractical and irrelevant? What in the world does the doctrine of the Trinity have to do with my relationship with my wife or coworker? The reason it seems jarring to inject God and theology into a discussion about human relationships is because we commonly misunderstand theology. We see theology as a systematic study of religious thought that has little to do with everyday life. But, rightly understood, theology is the real life story of God's relationship to us and our relationship to one another lived out in a broken world. By this definition, whether you "think" theologically or not, you are "doing" theology every day in the decisions you make, the words you speak, the feelings you have, and the attitudes you nurture in your heart. All of these responses are rooted in your perspective on the nature of God, yourself, your relationships, and the world around you. These "perspectives" are theology because they inform and frame the way you live your life. The question is not whether you are a theologian, but what kind of theologian you are!

All people assemble a set of "facts" that they believe are true. These facts function as a lens that is used to interpret life and relationships. The Bible is the only reliable source for these life-interpreting facts. The ultimate fact is the existence of God. Because we were made in God's likeness, we cannot talk about the nature of human relationships without first thinking about the nature of God. The biblical story presents us with a God who is three persons in one. This is the foundation for understanding what it means to be made in the image of God and fully human. John 17:20–26 shows the way the Bible connects God's nature with ours and his purpose for us. It is even more poignant as Jesus's prayer for his people as he contemplates his death.

> "My prayer is not for them alone. I pray also for those who will believe in me through their message, that all of them may be one, Father, just as you are in me and I am in you. May they also be in us so that the world may believe that you have sent me. I have given them the glory that you gave me, that they may be one as we are one: I in them and you in me. May they be brought to complete unity to let the world know that you sent me and have loved them even as you have loved me.

"Father, I want those you have given me to be with me where I am, and to see my glory, the glory you have given me because you loved me before the creation of the world.

"Righteous Father, though the world does not know you, I know you, and they know that you have sent me. I have made you known to them, and will continue to make you known in order that the love you have for me may be in them and that I myself may be in them."

As Jesus looks back on his public ministry and all it was meant to accomplish and forward to the cross and all it was ordained to produce, his focus is riveted on community! Of all the things Christ could pray for at this moment, he prays for the unity of his people. Let's consider the assumptions that are the basis for Christ's prayer and the framework for relationships.

God is the only properly functioning community in the universe

As Jesus communes with the Father, he reflects on the relationship that Father, Son, and Spirit have had for all eternity. He longs for his people to experience the same things in our community with God and one another. Christ's words echo the realities present in the Genesis account of the creation of humanity. As Anthony A. Hoekema says, "The first thing that strikes us as we look at Genesis 1:26 is that the main verb is in the plural: 'Then God said, "Let us make man."'"[2] We are given a glimpse into the divine community as Father, Son, and Spirit commit to make the human community in the image of the triune God. John 17 brings greater clarity of God's design given in Genesis 1:26 by describing the intimate unity God intends and its purposes. It gives insight into Christ's design and function for the church. God knows how to help us with our struggles with community because he is a community.

The Trinity is the only adequate model for human community

When Jesus reflects on God's purpose for human community, the only adequate pattern he can find is the community between Father,

---

2   Anthony A. Hoekema, *Created in God's Image* (Grand Rapids: Eerdmans, 1986), 12. While there are other aspects to what it means for humanity to be in God's image, the emphasis in this passage is on God as a divine community creating a human community.

Son, and Spirit. In essence he is saying, "Father, the only example of the community we have designed for our people is the community we have experienced together." When our relationships aren't working as they were designed, we can look to this model.

Does it surprise you that God presents himself as a model for human community? It can be surprising because we tend to think of God as an individual. While God is one, the Bible also says that he exists in three persons.

The biblical teaching of the Trinity is very practical for relationships since God himself is a model of loving, cooperative, unified community where diversity is an asset, not a liability. If God is making us into his likeness, we can be encouraged that he will give us the grace to live like this in community with one another.

People made in God's likeness were made for community

Christ's prayer reflects God's word in Genesis 2:18 as he looks at his glorious creation before the fall: "It is not good for the man to be alone." Human community was not only Christ's plan for his disciples; it was also God's plan for all people from the very beginning. Even though we are flawed people in flawed relationships, we are created to be social beings. Community with one another is not just a duty; it is an aspect of our humanity.

God has a two-fold purpose for human community: personal growth and witness to the world

Christ's prayer is that his people would grow and reflect his glory to a watching world. The ultimate flaw in the three kinds of relationships described earlier is that each is driven by personal desire rather than God's purposes. As we live together, we must always keep the bigger agenda of God's glory in view. Our relationships must be shaped not by what we want, but by what God intends.

Sin's self-centeredness cuts us off from God and others

Jesus would not be praying for us and moving toward the cross if we could manufacture this kind of community on our own. In John 17:17, he prays for our growth. Christ's starting point is the same as the apostle Paul's in 2 Corinthians 5:14–15—that sin turns us inward, away from God's grace and others: "For Christ's love compels us, because we are convinced that one died for all, and therefore all died. And he died for all, that those who live should no longer live for themselves but for him who died for them and was raised again." The night I imagined being single revealed a shocking selfishness in me. I wanted life to be comfortable, predictable, and easy. I wanted that because I thought that would be best for me.

True human community only arises out of communion with God

Jesus's language on this point is striking. He welcomes us into this divine community with Father, Son, and Spirit so that we can experience community with one another. That evening in the grocery store parking lot, my problem was not just that I didn't love my family as I should. My problem was that I didn't love God as I should. That weakened my love for my family. My panic was about more than being overwhelmed in my responsibilities; it revealed a lack of trust in God. We can't move toward community with one another until we have been drawn into community with God. The image here is of two concentric circles of relationship as opposed to two separate circles. The circle of human community can only thrive within the larger circle of community with God. Jesus prays that we would know that the Father's love for us is the same as his love for Jesus! (John 17:23). What a welcome into divine community!

Think of it as illustrated in Figure 3-2.

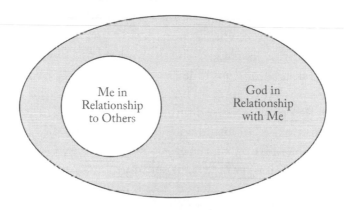

Figure 3-2

Christ's resolve confirms the commitment made by Father, Son, and Spirit before the creation of the world

Jesus is not manufacturing a new idea for human relationships or the church. His prayer reflects what God's design has always been. I had become discouraged as a father and a husband because I had lost sight of God's design. People made in God's likeness will reflect that likeness and glory only when they live in committed community. As Jesus looks to the cross and the ultimate defeat of sin, he knows that his death and resurrection will not only reconcile individual sinners to God, but also individual sinners to one another. Jesus's death and resurrection create an entirely new community that will come to full expression in eternity. (See Ephesians 2:11–22.)

God will dwell in community with his people so that they can know community with one another

As Jesus prays, he knows that the guilt of sin separates us from God and others. That is why he goes to the cross. But he is also aware that the ongoing presence of sin will make living in community impossible if we are not empowered in an ongoing way. John 17:22 is significant because the glory Jesus is talking about is the glory of the Holy Spirit, which allowed him to minister in a fallen world. He gives this same glory-Spirit to us because without the Spirit we can do nothing.

That night in my car, I had not properly measured my potential. My potential to be successful at what God had called me to do was not based on my track record or my responsibilities. It was tied to the grace given to me in Christ. Jesus would give me all I needed to live with my family. Jesus faced the unthinkable so I would have the power to live in relationships of love.

Do you see what is going on here? As Jesus prays to the Father for the creation of a new human community, he is anticipating what will happen to his own relationship with his Father as he dies to bear the sins of his people. His cry on the cross, "My God, my God, why have you forsaken me?" is a cry of broken communion among the members of the Trinity. The perfect, eternal love relationship between Father, Son, and Spirit was ripped apart to allow us to be restored to God and reconciled to one another.

The Image of God Is a Community

When you look at the various stages of a person's life, what do you observe? We are dependent on our mothers from the moment of conception. As soon as we're born, we need our family's care to survive. Even as we grow more self-sufficient, we still seek out human companionship. As teenagers we desire the acceptance of our peers and begin to experience the pull towards deeper, longer lasting, and more committed relationships. As adults we live in a variety of intersecting communities: family, church, neighborhood, and work. As we get older, we look back on our lives and remember the web of relationships that has been ours. Our fondest memories and deepest hurts involve relationships. Finally, one of our saddest moments is when death robs us of a loved one.

What does this survey of a person's life demonstrate? Despite the fact that we are selfish people in a fallen world, our lives still reveal God's likeness. God is a community and we as his creation reflect this quality. Moreover, he brings us into community and places the desire for community within us. Ultimately, we can never escape our essential nature—who and what God designed us to be. This relational characteristic is central to who we are; it leads us to do great good and great evil. This was demonstrated by the terrorism and heroism that took place simultaneously on September 11, 2001. The hatred of one community for another led to death and destruction; but the love other people had for their community produced amazing acts of courage, kindness, and self-sacrifice.

What does all this biblical and experiential data tell us? That you cannot talk about human beings made in God's image without talking about relationships. Yet it is often the first thing we overlook. Only when human beings live in community do we fully reflect the likeness of God.

Are You Denying Your Humanity?

Are relationships optional for you? The arguments from Scripture and daily life say, "Absolutely not!" If my identity as a human being is tied to community, then to deny, avoid, escape, misuse, exploit, or destroy it is to deny my own humanity. You deny your humanity every time you avoid someone, when you get angry with your children, when you opt for isolation over facing your hurt, when you exploit another human being, or when you give way to bigotry. James 3:9 says, "With the tongue we praise our Lord and Father, and with it we curse men, who have been made in God's likeness." Whenever you curse another person, you are destroying the thing you were both created for: God-shaped community. Ultimately, you are cursing the God who made the person, which means you have denied not only another's humanity, but your own as well.

In contrast, every time you move toward someone in compassion, you affirm your humanity. You do this every time you care about someone else's story as much as your own, seek or grant forgiveness, or function as a peacemaker. Every time you affirm the humanity of another, you honor the Creator who made you both. Because of the coexistence of sin and grace, we all shift between denying and affirming our humanity. One moment you are comforting your child and the next you are gossiping on the phone! In an attempt to serve someone, you argue with your spouse about the best way to accomplish your good deed!

John Calvin said, "For errors can never be uprooted from human hearts until a true knowledge of God is planted therein."[3] If there are problems in your relationships, the solution starts with God. Typically, we start with what we want. But starting with yourself and your own perceived wants and needs will bring you into collision with another person doing the same thing. It will doom the relationship. Only no options when we start with God—someone bigger than ourselves—can we escape the destructive results of our own selfishness. Human relationships are most satisfying when we enter them not just to please ourselves or even the other person, but to please God. The circle of human community is only healthy when it exists within the larger circle of community with God.

---

3   John Calvin, *The Institutes of the Christian Religion*, Vol. 1 (Philadelphia: Westminster Press, 1960), 73.

4

Sin

The LORD saw how great man's wickedness on the earth had
become, and that every inclination of the thoughts of his heart
was only evil all the time. The Lord was grieved that he had
made man on the earth, and his heart was filled with pain.

Genesis 6:5–6

Kristin and Shane had been friends since grade school. In high
school something more than friendship began to blossom.
Although they ended up at different colleges, they remained close
and spent at least three weekends a month together.

It wasn't long before they began to talk about marriage. They felt
so fortunate to marry someone who had been a friend since childhood!
The college years flew by and soon after graduation they married. They
looked forward to spending the rest of their lives together.

Shane and Kristin got good jobs and purchased a beautiful home
in a neighborhood they loved. Their days were busy, but their eve-
nings together were wonderful. They always looked forward to their
Saturday brunch at the bohemian café down the street. It seemed like
they were living their dream when, unexpectedly, Kristin began to
feel sick. Her doctor gave her the shocking news that she was pregnant. She had tried to be so careful! This was not part of the plan.
What in the world would she tell Shane?

Kristin dreaded seeing Shane and answering the question he was
sure to ask. She wanted him to be understanding, maybe even excited,

but she knew this was unlikely. That conversation was a turning point in their relationship. Shane was very upset that Kristin "hadn't been more careful." Kristin was crushed that Shane would blame the pregnancy on her and treat the baby like a disease. On top of this, Kristin and Shane desperately needed her income; but if she continued to be as sick as she had been, she wouldn't be able to work for long. Shane was discouraged, Kristin was sick, and their finances were growing tighter every day.

Their struggles soon began to erode their relationship. Shane became bitter and frustrated. He had been raised in a well-managed, financially stable family. He was irritated that they had gotten themselves into such a tight spot. Kristin was hurt that her closest friend now seemed like her worst enemy. Together they wondered how their marriage had become such a mess.

In the Middle of the Mess

Your best relationship—no matter who it's with—is messy! Stop and think about your most satisfying relationship. (If you are having difficulty, we have proven our point.) Ask yourself these simple questions about this relationship:

- Have you ever felt misunderstood?
- Have you ever been hurt by what the other person said?
- Have you ever felt like you haven't been heard?
- Have you ever been betrayed?
- Have you ever had to work through a misunderstanding?
- Have you ever disagreed on a decision?
- Have you or the other person ever held a grudge?
- Have you ever experienced loneliness even when things were going well?
- Have you ever been let down?
- Have you ever doubted the other person's love?
- Has the other person ever doubted your commitment?
- Have you ever struggled to resolve a conflict?
- Have you ever wished you didn't have to give or serve?
- Have you ever felt used?
- Have you ever thought, *If I had only known!*

Do these questions reveal underlying struggles and temptations in your best relationship? In our case, our best relationships are with our wives (which is ideal, but not always the case). Both of us have been married for many years, and we consider our marriages to be strong and loving. We are married to women we greatly respect, and our marriages have benefited from God's wisdom and grace. Even so, both of us could answer "yes" to every question listed above, and we are certain our wives would say the same.

It is not hard to understand James's question in James 4:1: "What causes fights and quarrels among you?" Your experience in relationships helps you understand why the Bible includes so many commands and exhortations to be patient, kind, forgiving, compassionate, gentle, and humble. The Bible assumes that relationships this side of eternity will be messy and require a lot of work. If this applies to our *best* relationships, how much more does it apply to relationships that are more difficult!

Inside, Outside, Upside Down

It is tempting to look at the trouble in our relationships and locate the problem outside ourselves. And it's true: the other person *is* inherently weak and sinful! Unfortunately, so are we. James 4:1 (with the rest of Scripture) reminds us that our real problem is inside us. We have all made a decision to turn things upside down. What we want, for ourselves and from others, becomes more important to us than God himself. We have made ourselves ultimate and God secondary. The Bible calls this sin, as we reject God's rightful rule over us and decide to become our own ruler. When we do this, our selfish desires go on to rule our relationships, leading to problems, conflict, and disappointment with others.

The apostle Paul describes his biggest problem as an internal one in Romans 7:21–25:

> So I find this law at work: When I want to do good, evil is right there with me. For in my inner being I delight in God's law; but I see another law at work in the members of my body, waging war against the law of my mind and making me a prisoner of the law of sin at work within my

members. What a wretched man I am! Who will rescue me from this body of death? Thanks be to God—through Jesus Christ our Lord!

So then, I myself in my mind am a slave to God's law, but in the sinful nature a slave to the law of sin.

Paul uses four helpful terms to describe his experience:

1. The term *law* explains an inescapable principle at work in his life. That principle is like gravity: you can't choose to be free from its influence. Until you are finally delivered from the power and presence of sin, you will never escape your own sin in relationships.
2. The term *war* illustrates the ever-present struggle going on within Paul. This inner conflict, between a desire to do what is right and the power of sin, is still at work.
3. The term *prisoner* describes the experience of the redeemed sinner. Have you ever wanted to do the right thing, but instead were pulled into sin? You said to yourself, *I can't believe I did that again!* This is what it feels like to be a prisoner. A prisoner has lost his freedom.
4. The word *rescue* is a dramatic word that is often overlooked in these verses, though in light of the three previous words, it should shine even more brightly. When you need rescue, it means you are hopeless without outside help.

These four words mean that *our biggest problem is inside us and we can't fix it on our own.* Paul's evaluation of the struggle with sin is sobering, as it calls our attention to its impact on our relationships. Sin affects us in six basic ways.

Self-Centeredness

When you reject God, you create a void that cannot remain empty. Sin will lead you instinctively to fill it with yourself. When things got tough for Kristin and Shane, they immediately defaulted to a "What is best for me?" position, rather than a "What is God doing in and through us?" perspective. Since relationships are about being other-centered, the self-centeredness of sin will inevitably subvert God's design. And since both people will be struggling with the same thing, it's easy to see the conflicts that can and will result. ("I thought I was important to you" vs. "I was just trying to protect my rights.")

Self-Rule

When God's wise and loving rule over you is replaced with self-rule, other people become your subjects. They are expected to do your bidding and bow to your control. How do Kristin and Shane respond to each other in difficulty? They take control. Shane tries to dominate Kristin with criticism and demands; Kristin tries to control Shane with isolation and silence. But because relationships are supposed to be conducted between two people who are equally submitted to God, the quest for self-rule will always wreak havoc. ("If you really loved me, you would do the things that please me.")

Self-Sufficiency

When you reject God, you believe the intoxicating but poisonous delusion that you are not dependent. In Kristin and Shane's case, the problem is not just the unexpected circumstances they are facing. Their circumstances are difficult, but God has not left them alone. He has given them himself and each other. But in moving away from each other, they are moving away from one of God's principal means of providing for them. If you don't see that you are dependent upon God, it is unlikely that you will be humbly dependent on others. Relationships are best built upon godly, mutual dependence. The redemptive give-and-take God uses to show his love for us is missing when independence rules. ("If I need your help, I'll ask for it. I like our friendship; I just don't like your help.")

Self-Righteousness

When the holiness of God is not your personal standard of what is good, true, and right, you will always set *yourself* up as that standard. This is what happened to Kristin and Shane. Each thinks he or she is more righteous than the other. Each is very aware of the other's sin and working hard to get the other to see it too. Meanwhile, neither is looking at his or her own heart, owning personal weakness and sin and seeking the help that only Jesus can provide. This approach will invariably lead you to develop an inflated view of yourself and, by necessity, an overly critical view of others. Godly relationships flourish best between two humble people who acknowledge their weaknesses and sins and their need for grace. The self-righteous person who denies his own need will not be a channel of grace to others. ("After all I have done for you, this is the way you treat me?!")

Self-Satisfaction

When you convince yourself that satisfaction and fulfillment can be found apart from God, you can move in two different directions. Kristin and Shane are both guilty here. Kristin has replaced (with her girlfriends) the community God wants her to have with Shane. Shane has put his energies and hope into his job. Neither is making the investments in the relationship they once loved to make. Notice the dynamic here. If you find satisfaction in material things, you will either be disinterested in relationships or use them to get what you want. If you find satisfaction in people, you will use relationships for your own happiness. ("This is not what I expected out of this relationship. If I had known this was going to happen, I would never have begun.")

Self-Taught

When you are your own source of truth and wisdom, you forsake the humble, teachable spirit that is vital to a good relationship. You will always be the mentor in your relationships and give the impression that you have little if anything to learn from others. ("I don't need you to tell me what to do!") The shocking thing in Kristin and Shane's story is how quickly they stopped listening to one another.

Figure 4-1 summarizes the effects these kinds of sins have on a person and his relationships. If you see yourself in many of these categories, that is not unusual. Take heart: this diagnosis, though hard to swallow, can lead to real change as you see how much you need God's grace.

	Seeks/ Wants	Acceptable Cost	Nightmare/ Fear	Others' Experience	Telltale Emotion/ Action
Self-Centeredness	Attention, approval	Will sacrifice control and independence	Rejection, not being recognize or affirmed	Others feel used, minimized, smothered	Anxious, needy
Self-Rule	To be right, in control	Will sacrifice intimacy and unity	Being seen as wrong, being dependent	Others feel coerced, manipulated	Angry
Self-Sufficiency	Independence, time alone	Will sacrifice intimacy, mutually helpful community	The dependence and neediness of others	Others feel ignored, unappreciated	Cold, distant
Self-Righteousness	Being right in the eyes of others	Will sacrifice relationships that challenge or confront	Being wrong, guilty, or condemned	Others feel challenged, condemned, or dismissed	Aggressive, argumentative
Self-Satisfaction	Pleasure (self-defined)	Will sacrifice community if inconvenient	Others interfering with personal pleasure	Others feel like objects, not companions	Controlling, demanding, dissatisfied
Self-Taught	A platform for one's own opinion	Will sacrifice growing together if you disagree	Being told what to think, say, and do	Others feel patronized, disrespected	Opinionated, domineering

Figure 4-1

Because sin turns us inward, there is a Kristin and a Shane in us all. When love for God is replaced by love for self, we see people either as obstacles that hinder our goals or vehicles that promote them. Sinful self-interest turns the two great commands upside down: rather than loving God and using his gifts to serve others, we love the gifts and use people to get them. For example, parents who crave a good reputation view their children as tools to gain it. Spouses who crave intimacy manipulate their mates to get it. People who crave success view others as either a means or a threat to their agenda. People who crave comfort are excited about easy relationships and annoyed by difficult ones. People who crave control are threatened by strength and gravitate to weakness. People who crave material things shun relationships that hinder their pursuit.

Do you see what happens when something other than the living God rules your heart? There is no way to get around the profound truth in James 4:1. Whenever the things you want become more important than God, your relationships suffer. Even when you make *relationships* more important than God, your relationships suffer! This is what sin does. It blinds us to our dependence upon God, turns us inward, and causes us to either fear or exploit others.

In chapter 2, we said that the circle of human relationships was meant only to exist within the larger circle of community with God. In this context, all relationships are shaped by an allegiance to God, and they thrive and grow. Sin, however, places human community within the context of an allegiance to other gods (comfort, control, material things, power, success, approval). This radically alters the agenda we have for other people. In this context, my affection for other people is never an end in itself, but a means to an end: getting what I want.

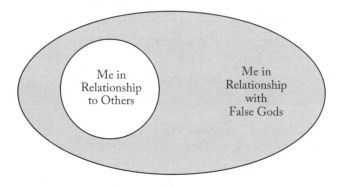

Figure 4-2

What about the Bad Things People Do to Me?

This is a fair question. It is not only fair, but also good and wise. What we have said so far may give the impression that your relationships are only harmed by *your* sin. But the Bible is a very realistic book. It takes into account that you are also sinned against. Like Shane, you are sometimes the victimizer and need to deal with your sin. And like Kristin, you are sometimes the victim. And there are times when you are both! Without a doubt, the victimizer needs to face his sin, yet the victim is still responsible for his response to being sinned against.

The Bible is filled with examples that deal honestly with victimization, from the murder of Abel in Genesis 4 to the persecution of the church in Revelation. There are countless stories of people sinning against each other. The New Testament is full of exhortations calling us to exercise patience, forbearance, and compassion, to revoke revenge and anger, to forgive others and love our enemies. The Bible mentions these things because God knows we will be sinned against frequently. Here on earth, we will always be sinners relating to other sinners.

Therefore, even when we are sinned against, we are responsible for how we react. This is the only way we can turn back the destructive power of sin in a relationship. Micah 6:8 gives us direction regarding our reactions to sin: "He has showed you, O man, what is good. And what does the LORD require of you? To act justly and to love mercy and to walk humbly with your God." Why would this instruction be necessary if it did not presuppose that we would be sinned against? This is important because we all tend to sin in response to being sinned against. We tend to add trouble to our trouble! Some of the typical ways we do this are as follows:

- I confess your sins to myself with bitterness. *I can't believe she did that to me!*
- I confess your sins to another person in gossip. "Let me tell you what she did to me!"
- I confess your sins to God, seeking vengeance. "God, when are you going to do something to the person who hurt me?"
- I confess your sins to you in anger. "How dare you do such a thing to me?"

When it comes to the sins others commit against us, we tend to communicate about them in destructive ways. This is wrong, and it encourages us to think that our biggest problem is outside ourselves. The Bible reminds us that even when we are sinned against, ultimately, before God our biggest problem is still our own hearts' propensity to sin. Even when our hearts have been horribly damaged by the sins of another, we are to guard our hearts so that we are not sucked into sin's destructiveness. Being sinned against tempts us to sin. So our need for Christ is as big when we are sinned against as it is when we sin. The calls to patience, humility, forgiveness, and gentleness are not calls to passivity. God is calling you to respond, but as he prescribes it. Holding grudges, becoming bitter, praying for vengeance, and gossiping are not methods that God honors. When you hold the perpetrator "accountable," but not in a spirit of humility, patience, and compassion, you end up perverting the very justice you seek.

There Is Grace for This Struggle!

Is it hard for you to read this chapter without being overwhelmed by the messiness of relationships? Maybe you are saying, "Find me an island where I can live alone!" What will keep Kristin and Shane from going there? What will give them hope to move toward each other in patient love again? We have said that some of the worst and best experiences of life happen in relationships. We have spoken at length about why some of the worst things have happened. But why have some of your *best* experiences been in the very same context? Have you ever wondered why you have had any *good* relationships?

Every good relationship we have is a gift of God's grace. Left to ourselves, nothing good would happen! God's grace is the reason why a mom who struggles with selfishness can also exhibit genuine care for her children. It's why a self-absorbed husband can serve his wife when she becomes ill. Have you ever wondered how two non-Christians can have a reasonably good relationship? It is because the very God they deny is showing them his grace and blessing despite their ignorance.

Think of what God has given to help us navigate relationships in a fallen world. He has given his *Word*, which is rich with wise principles. He has given us his *Spirit*, who convicts us when we are wrong, empowers us to seek forgiveness, and enables us to show compassion to those who have wronged us. He has given us a community of *fellow Christians*, where we receive ongoing correction and encouragement.

Two often-overlooked provisions are the *sacraments* of baptism and the Lord's Supper. Each embodies all of these blessings in a single act. They picture our dependence on grace, as well as our dependence on one another to grow in grace. Baptism is a sign declaring my relationship with God and my inclusion into the people of God. The Lord's Supper unites us all around one table. It is a picture of a family gathering and a shared meal. These things are more than just symbols; they are actually means of grace. God gives us his grace through them when we participate by faith. Our mistake is to think of grace as deliverance from problems; in reality, it is the ability to persevere in the midst of those problems. We desire the "grace"of relief while God gives us the true grace of empowerment.

We make a mistake when we measure our potential to deal with difficulty by the size and duration of the problem. We should be measuring our potential according to the size of God's provision and the promise of his eternal presence. Even in the deepest difficulty, we are never without resources. We are never alone. This is a profound and radical way to think about relationships. Our problems have everything to do with sin, and our potential has everything to do with Christ. Our goal in this book is to hold onto both. While sin is an ever-present reality, it is no match for Jesus Christ! We hope you will become more realistic (and less fearful) about the struggle of relationships, while gaining a more hopeful grasp of the grace God gives for that struggle.

Shane and Kristin did find grace for their struggle. When they decided to seek help, it was hard at first. It was devastating to listen to the other talk about their hurts. It was discouraging to see how far and how fast they had drifted apart. But as they faced these tough realities, they also saw something else. They began to see their God— not off in the distance somewhere, but right there with them in the difficulty. As they began to trust him, they began to find the courage to trust each other again. And because they had already experienced God's help, they continued to move toward each other, knowing that his help would be available whenever they needed it again.

5

Agendas

"No one can serve two masters. Either he will hate the one and love the other, or he will be devoted to the one and despise the other. You cannot serve both God and Money."

Matthew 6:24

As you read the following statements, see if you can pick out the underlying agenda:

- "I am so happy we don't argue like we used to."
- "I just love being with you."
- "I'm enjoying the time I am spending with my family."
- "I am so thankful for my friends."
- "You've been so good to me."
- "It's great to know that I have found someone I can
- truly trust."
- "We're such kindred spirits."
- "It's wonderful how our personalities are so complementary."
- "This has been fun; let's get together again."
- "We have such a great sex life."
- "Before I met you, I was so lonely."
- "It's great we have known each other for so long."
- "We've had so many nice times together."
- "We've had our problems, but we have always been able to work through them."

Who wouldn't want to be able to say these things about his relationships? All of these things are good. But what is the agenda in each of these statements? It's what the person gets out of the relationship. For all of us as self-centered people, this agenda for personal happiness is very seductive. Sin always draws us toward self-interest. It is possible that even our most altruistic moments are driven by what we get out of them.

A wealthy celebrity has just given a sizable donation to a worthy cause. During an interview he is asked, "What motivated you to make this donation?" At first glance the gift seems to be a generous act of kindness. But the celebrity's answer has a different slant. "When I wake up in the morning, I can look at myself in the mirror and say that I am a good person. And when I go to bed at night, I can feel good about myself." No doubt the donation will benefit others no matter what the celebrity's motive, but the point is that what looks good on the surface doesn't always look that way under closer inspection.

What the Scriptures say about relationships is utterly unique. These two themes predominate.

The power of self-interest is still present in the believer

While the control of sin has been broken, the sin that remains in us still puts up a real fight. This means that while you live on earth, you will not fully escape the power of self-interest in your life. It will remain a reality even in your best relationships. In fact, the more satisfying the relationship, the less conscious you will be of self-interest. The most destructive diseases are the ones that don't show themselves in obvious ways. This is true of spiritual maladies as well.

God has a bigger agenda for our relationships than we do

The default questions we ought to bring to every area of life should be, "What is God's purpose and design? What was his reason for creating this?" When we apply these questions to relationships, we begin to see how different his agenda is from our own. We would easily settle for our own definition of personal happiness when God's purpose is nothing short of conforming us to the image of Christ! Whether we are conscious of it or not, we all have dreams for our relationships, and we are always working to realize those dreams. How close is your dream to God's purpose?

This chapter will compare your dream with God's dream for your relationships. We all live somewhere between the two. The best thing you can do is become more conscious of which one rules you. To help you do this, we offer a Scriptural template to help you assess your relationships.

A Road Map to a Bigger Agenda

Our template or road map is Ephesians 4. As you read it, ask yourself what it says about (1) the struggle of self-interest and (2) God's agenda for our relationships. This passage will be the grid you can use to look at the issues of relationship we address in this book.

As you consider this passage, think about Elise, Kurt, Kristin, and Shane. While you're at it, think about yourself too. Why do we get angry? Why are we impatient? Why do we fail to be kind and gentle? Why do we hold a grudge or act out of vengeance? Why do we refuse to cooperate? Why do we say things to one another that should never be uttered? Why do we walk away in disgust? Why would we lie to someone or seek to manipulate? Why are we competitive and envious? Why do we struggle to rejoice at another's blessing? We do all of these things for one reason: *We want our own way, in the way we have chosen, and at the time we have deemed best.* We love us and we have a wonderful plan for our lives! We have a dream. The problem is that it is not the Lord's.

A Call to Unity

> As a prisoner for the Lord, then, I urge you to live a life worthy of the calling you have received. Be completely humble and gentle; be patient, bearing with one another in love. Make every effort to keep the unity of the Spirit through the bond of peace. There is one body and one Spirit—just as you were called to one hope when you were called—one Lord, one faith, one baptism; one God and Father of all, who is over all and through all and in all. (Ephesians 4:1–6)

Josh and Sara moved their family of six to a completely new area two months ago. The opportunity for a promotion, a bigger house, and a nicer climate ruled the day. There was little thought to the spiritual impact the move might have on their family. They did a quick search on the internet for local churches, but only after the decision to move had already been made. Although it is certainly not wrong to move or take a promotion, Josh and Sara were driven by a comfortable life-style, not God's will. In their decision-making process, little thought was given to the importance of connecting with a body of believers where they could invest in the lives of others and others woulddo the same for them. Their decision ignored who God had made them to be and how he had designed them to live in community.

After a lengthy discussion on the grace of God, Paul applies that grace to our relationships in Ephesians 4. Verse 1 urges us to live a life "worthy of the calling [we] have received." You are a recipient of grace and your life should reflect that! Specifically, Paul says it should show up in our relationships within the body of Christ. In other words, you can't take the gospel seriously and not take your relationships seriously. But we tend to make compromises that negatively impact our relationships without seeing the contradiction.

Look at what Paul believes and expects the grace of God to do in our relationships. As you read the following list, ask yourself if this is how you think about your relationships. It may be helpful to use this list to think about one particular relationship.

Maintain the unity of the Spirit

Paul says that our relationships with other Christians are not something we should take for granted. He says that we are to *maintain*—not *create*—these relationships. If you are a Christian, you automatically are in relationship with other Christians. You are united to one another because you are united to Christ. Because of the indwelling of the Holy Spirit, you already share a deep bond that has been given to you by grace. Therefore, these relationships are gifts to be managed with great care. I am either being a good or a bad steward of these gifts. If I hinder my relationships with other believers in any way, I am devaluing these relationships. If I gossip or engage in ungodly conflict, I harm the gift God has given. But if I am willing to pursue, forgive, and serve, I demonstrate care for these gifts.

Make every effort

Paul is not naïve about the hard work relationships require. He knows that relationships, even among people who have the Spirit, will not be easy. Have you ever noticed how distasteful, unsatisfying, and uninteresting relationships suddenly become when they require work? How many marriages have suffered because neither husband nor wife had a biblical work ethic for their relationship? Paul says that we find excitement and satisfaction within the context of hard work. But most of us give up when we decide that the dividend yield is not worth the investment. Sadly, we frequently do the accounting with our personal interests at the center instead of God's call.

Be humble, gentle, patient, and forbearing in love

Paul leads with character qualities that are the opposite of what often drive our relationships. It is important to note that these are character qualities before they are actions toward others. Humility enables us to see our own sin before we focus on the sin and weaknesses of another. *Do you hold others to a higher standard than you do yourself?* A gentle person is not weak, but someone who uses his strength to empower others. A gentle person can use strength without damaging those he is trying to help. *Do people regularly feel bruised in their relationship with you?* A patient person is someone who places the needs of others higher than, or at the same level as, his own. He doesn't come with a self-centered agenda. A forbearing person is someone who does all this even when provoked. In other words, people who are patient and forbearing are humble and gentle even when they are provoked or when the investment they have made in a relationship turns sour. *Do you love people with limits that are driven by your own perceived needs or interests? Do others feel as if they must always return a favor to keep you happy with them?*

These character qualities create a climate of grace for relationships. Usually, relationships are governed by a structure of law, offense, and punishment. I have a set of rules you must abide by. I am watching to make sure you follow these rules. If you don't, I feel justified in mering out some form of punishment. This is a flagrant contradiction of the gospel, and it prevents the glory and worth of God's grace from showing itself in your relationships. This is the exact opposite of what Paul says should be true of those who receive grace.

There is one Spirit, one Lord, and one Father

Paul grounds our unity in the unity of the Trinity, not in our ability to get along. We get along because Father, Son, and Spirit have allowed us to do so. We can give grace because we have been given grace. Jesus humbled himself. The Father gently and patiently works out our salvation. The Holy Spirit forbears and abides with us even in the face of our sin, convicting and correcting us, but never condemning. Father, Son, and Spirit were torn apart so that we might be united with them and with each other.

This kind of relational integrity is a high calling, but the God who commands it provides us with everything we need to fulfill it. What if Josh and Sara had had this perspective on their potential relocation? Christian relationships would have been a priority instead of an afterthought.

An Appreciation of Diversity

But to each one of us grace has been given as Christ apportioned it. This is why it says:

"When he ascended on high, he led captives in his train and gave gifts to men."

(What does "he ascended" mean except that he also descended to the lower, earthly regions? He who descended is the very one who ascended higher than all the heavens, in order to fill the whole universe.) It was he who gave some to be apostles, some to be prophets, some to be evangelists, and some to be pastors and teachers, to prepare God's people for works of service, so that the body of Christ may be built up until we all reach unity in the faith and in the knowledge of the Son of God and become mature, attaining to the whole measure of the fullness of Christ.

Then we will no longer be infants, tossed back and forth by the waves, and blown here and there by every wind of teaching and by the cunning and craftiness of men in their deceitful scheming. Instead, speaking the truth in love, we will in all things grow up into him who is the Head, that is, Christ. From him the whole body, joined and held together by every supporting ligament, grows and builds itself up in love, as each part does its work. (Ephesians 4:7–16)

Because it is grounded in the Trinity, our unity also allows us to celebrate our diversity in the body of Christ. There is one God, but three persons. God uses our diversity to accomplish his purpose—our growth in grace. Diversity is not an obstacle, but a very significant means to this end.

But to each one of us grace has been given as Christ apportioned it

Notice all the differences that exist among us. We have different gifts, serve in different capacities in the body of Christ, and are at various levels of spiritual maturity. All of these differences are there by God's sovereign apportionment. That is, God chooses to surround us with people who are different from us because he knows it will promote his purpose. Yet how often do we see diversity as a hindrance to good relationships and God's purposes?

So that the body of Christ may be built up

We see God's purpose throughout verses 12–16. Over and over, Paul argues that our relationships are valuable because God has a purpose for them. Whenever we try to give our relationships purpose, we become impatient, frustrated, and exploitative. And since we are all sinners, we will always thwart each other's purposes. This dynamic begins to reveal why God has put us in relationships. Our purpose is to get what we want, but God's purpose is to give us what we really need. God ultimately wants us to mature, to be built up, and to stop acting like infants. He wants the things that ruled Christ's heart to rule ours as well.

This is where the true value of our relationships runs counter to what we normally think. We think things are going well only if we are getting along with others. But God says that it is also when we are not getting along with others that he is accomplishing his purposes! For example, if you quit at the first sign of fatigue when you exercise, you miss the chance to become more fit. Exercise after exhaustion is the most efficient and productive time for physical fitness. This is true of relationships as well. God has designed our relationships to function as both a diagnosis and a cure. When we are frustrated and ready to give up, God is at work, revealing the places where we have given in to a selfish agenda (the diagnosis). He then uses that new awareness to help us grow precisely where we have struggled (the cure). That is what the rest of this book is about.

We enter relationships for personal pleasure, self-actualization, and fun. We want low personal cost and high self-defined returns. But God wants high personal cost and high God-defined returns. And, although we frequently disagree with God, his plan is better. Beneath all our conflict with others lies a deeper conflict between these two agendas: ours and God's. When Josh and Sara decided to move, they did not consider these things at all. They treated relationships so lightly that they circumvented God's primary means of making them into the likeness of Christ. What seems like an innocent and obvious choice of career advancement actually became a hindrance to their growth in grace.

Our Struggle and God's Agenda

So I tell you this, and insist on it in the Lord, that you must no longer live as the Gentiles do, in the futility of their thinking. They are darkened in their understanding and separated from the life of God because of the ignorance that is in them due to the hardening of their hearts. Having lost all sensitivity, they have given themselves over to sensuality so as to indulge in every kind of impurity, with a continual lust for more.

You, however, did not come to know Christ that way. Surely you heard of him and were taught in him in accordance with the truth that is in Jesus. You were taught, with regard to your former way of life, to put off your old self, which is being corrupted by its deceitful desires; to be made new in the attitude of your minds; and to put on the new self, created to be like God in true righteousness and holiness.

Therefore each of you must put off falsehood and speak truthfully to his neighbor, for we are all members of one body. "In your anger do not sin": Do not let the sun go down while you are still angry, and do not give the devil a foothold. He who has been stealing must steal no longer, but must work, doing something useful with his own hands, that he may have something to share with those in need.

Do not let any unwholesome talk come out of your mouths, but only what is helpful for building others up according to their needs, that it may benefit those who listen. And do not grieve the Holy Spirit of God, with whom you were sealed for the day of redemption. Get rid of all bitterness, rage and anger, brawling and slander, along with every form of malice. Be kind and compassionate to one another, forgiving each other, just as in Christ God forgave you. (Ephesians 4:17–32)

Finally, Paul lays out what relationships look like when God's purpose rules. He identifies seven tendencies of the sinful heart that are damaging to relationships, disruptive of God's purpose, and require persistent battling. Ask yourself if any of them are evident in your relationships at home, at work, at church, in your extended family, or in your community.

The tendency toward self-indulgence (vv.19–24). My behavior in the relationship is driven by what I want, not God's purpose.

The tendency toward deceit (v. 25). I will manipulate the truth to get what I want out of the relationship.

The tendency toward anger (vv. 26–27). I want to control the relationship by venting my anger or by holding it over you to control you.

The tendency toward selfishness (v. 28). I want to protect what I have, rather than offer it to serve you.

The tendency toward unhelpful communication (vv. 29–30). Rather than use my speech to make you feel better and put you in a better position, I speak to make myself feel better and ensure that I am in the top spot.

The tendency toward division (v. 31). I give in to the temptation to view you as an adversary, rather than a companion in the struggle of relationship.

The tendency toward an unforgiving spirit (v. 32). I want to make others pay for their wrongs against me.

We are all tempted by these tendencies. We are not immune even as believers. Paul is writing to Christians because he assumes that these will be critical areas of struggle. The amazing part is that this entire passage promises grace for every area. One of the first places we see the evidence of God's grace personally is in the realization that relationships demand hard work. We become willing to enter the struggle rather than avoid it, because we start to see that this is where God is present and active. We begin to run toward others rather than away from them, and we begin to experience the following:

- How much wiser God's plan is for us than our plan for ourselves (vv. 19–24)
- The life-changing power of truthfulness (v. 25)
- The healing benefit of gentleness, patience, and love (vv. 26–27)
- The joy of serving the needs of someone else (v. 28)
- The value of loving and wholesome communication (vv. 29–30)
- The beauty of functional unity in a relationship (v. 31)
- The freedom of practicing forgiveness (v. 32)

What vision for relationships is the Bible painting for us? According to Ephesians 4, it is that the highest joys of relationship grow in the soil of the deepest struggles. Struggles are not obstacles, but instruments in God's hands. Every struggle is an opportunity to experience God's grace yourself and give it to the other person. Think about your relationships. Which are the most meaningful? Aren't they the ones that have lasted over time and have gone through excruciating difficulty? If you look at your own character, some of your deepest growth has been born out of great stress and trial.

As you end this chapter, be honest. What do you want out of your relationships? What do you want God to accomplish in those relationships? Will you settle for comfort, approval, ease, and happiness? Or are you willing to take up the biblical vision for relationships revealed in Ephesians 4? Your sanctification is at stake depending on how you answer this question.

Every day, in your relationships, you are pursuing one of these plans, driven by one of these two agendas: yours or God's. The plan you follow will shape your responses to everything you face in each relationship.

The rest of this book is about hard work, but it is the best work you will ever do. If you grow in these things, there will be obvious blessings. Your life and relationships will improve in many ways, but they will also get more complicated and messy. Because of this, you will come to see your need of God's grace even more. This is the exciting part!

6

Worship

With the tongue we praise our Lord and Father, and with it
we curse men, who have been made in God's likeness. Out of
the same mouth come praise and cursing. My brothers, this
should not be. Can both fresh water and salt water flow from
the same spring? My brothers, can a fig tree bear olives, or a
grapevine bear figs? Neither can a salt spring produce fresh
water.

James 3:9–12

Jenna just couldn't help herself; she was obsessed with Kelsey's opinion of her.

Lisa's constant focus on how neat their house was drove Jordan crazy.

Tamara was so driven to succeed in her new job, she had little time left for her new marriage.

Andy knew he spent too much time pointing out how spiritually immature Gwen was, but he couldn't get himself to stop.

It irritated Lindsey that Brandon could mess with his guitar all day when he never had time to read a book.

Tony didn't mind Celia's hospitality, but it bothered him that she left so little time for them as a couple.

Jason and Seth quit working together because they concluded they were too different to ever make it work.

It bugged John that Melanie could seem so spiritual yet be so theologically unaware.

It was a lot of little things: the crumpled tube of toothpaste, the toilet paper that was never on the roller, the butter left out on the counter, and the complete dismantling of the newspaper every night. These differences between Alfie and Jane really got on her nerves.

Tina sat in church with Chris, thinking that she could not imagine going there every Sunday after they were married.

Dwayne was convinced that he must have married the most unmechanical person who ever lived.

Ann was thankful for her friendship with Grace, but she was convinced that they would never be on the same page spiritually.

Everybody's Struggle, Everybody's Story

Can you relate to these struggles? Think about the people you encounter daily. Where do those relationships get difficult? Is there someone you love who also drives you crazy? Is there someone in your life you would like to rewire? Are there times when you experience a spiritual disconnect with a person you know and love? Are there times when someone's opinion of you becomes too important? Do you find yourself fighting over things that aren't that significant? Have you ever been shocked by a person's response to a certain situation? Have you ever thought it would be easier to be alone than to walk through the minefield of relationships?

Struggle in relationships is everyone's story. None of us has ever had a relationship completely free of struggle. All of us have had moments when we were discouraged by the effort a good relationship requires. Each of us has dreamed that those relationships would magically become easier. We've all wished for the power to change another person—and many of us have actually tried to remake someone in our own image. All of us have allowed inconsequential actions and habits to get under our skin and argued for a personal preference as if it were a moral absolute. And each of us has tried to be the Holy Spirit in another person's life, trying to work spiritual changes that only God can accomplish.

We have talked a little about why our relationships are so difficult and time-consuming. But what are the foundations of a healthy,

God-honoring relationship? What are the daily thoughts, desires, and habits that make a relationship good? Why *do* you struggle with one person one way and a different way with another?

We will start to look at those questions in this chapter. It is written out of the understanding that good relationships just don't drop out of the sky. Good relationships are built on a solid foundation. Without this foundation, no amount of hard work will make your relationships what God intended them to be.

The Two Foundation Stones

Matt and Rob didn't see what theology had to do with their problems working together. Their business venture had once been so exciting, but now it was fraught with conflict. They had a terrible time making decisions and an even worse time having the conversations that would lead to the decisions. Matt and Rob both tended to take their differences too personally; they felt like they were in an endless battle for control of the business. What they needed, they thought, was a "how to" manual on partnerships that would help them deal with each other. If such a book existed, they believed it would fix the problem. But they needed so much more.

Their true needs jumped out at them one week at their Bible study. They learned about two biblical concepts that not only helped them diagnose what was causing their problems, but also showed them the way out. This chapter traces their journey to reconciliation.

Good relationships are always built on the foundation stones of *identity* and *worship*. Even though these ideas may seem distant from our daily struggles, nothing can shelter our relationships from difficulty if we aren't building community on this foundation. We often mistakenly think that our relationships are difficult because, like a child learning to walk, we simply lack the skills and experience not to fall. This may be true in part, but the greater problem is the foundation we are walking on. For our relationships to be what God designed them to be, the rebuilding, restoring, and reconciling must start with a solid new foundation.

This foundation is not what we do and say. It begins in the heart, the source of the thoughts and motives that shape what we do and say. Your heart is always with you, and in profound ways it shapes your interactions with others. If our heart's foundation is solid, based on God's truth, design, and purpose for us, we will be able to build healthy, God-honoring relationships even though we are flawed people living in a broken world. By contrast, broken community is always the result of broken foundations.

The two stones in this foundation are identity and worship. When we talk about identity, we are not referring to your name, birth date, and Social Security number. We are talking about how you define yourself—what talents, qualities, experiences, achievements, goals, beliefs, relationships, and dreams you use to say, "This is who I am." Similarly, when we talk about worship, we do not simply mean the order of service at your church on Sunday morning. What we are getting at is that, because you are a human being, there is always something you are living for; always some desire, goal, treasure, purpose, value, or craving that controls your heart. The Bible reminds us that God wants—and deserves—to be the defining center of both these things.

When I live out of a biblical sense of *who I am* (identity) and rest in *who God is* (worship), I will be able to build a healthy relationship with you. These are not abstract theological concepts. We're talking about the content and character of our hearts. These foundational issues of identity and worship are an inescapable part of your nature as a human being. What you believe and do about these two things will shape the way you live with the people God has placed in your life. For this reason we can say that we all *live* theologically; that is, the things we believe about God and ourselves are the foundation for all the decisions we make, all the actions we take, and all the words we speak. The theology you live out is much more important to your daily life than the theology you claim to believe.

Remembering Who You Are

It is impossible for identity not to be an issue for human beings. God made us rational creatures who make choices based on the way we interpret life. One of the most important ways we try to make sense out of life is by telling ourselves who we are. We all have an "I am ___ _____, therefore I can _____" way of living. In God's plan, this quest for personal identity is meant to drive us back to him as Creator so that we find our meaning and purpose in him.

The identity I assign myself will always affect the way I respond to you. For example, if I tell myself that I am smarter than you, it will be hard for me to listen when you give me advice. If I tell myself that I deserve your respect, I will watch to see if you are giving me what I think I deserve. In ways like this, my sense of identity will always shape the way I think about my life and my relationships. This was happening to Matt and Rob, but they didn't know it.

Rob got his identity from success and achievement, but he constantly felt like Matt was in his way. Matt got his identity from the respect and acceptance of the people around him; he personalized all the disagreements he had with Rob. You can see how issues of identity were complicating this relationship.

A large part of the biblical story is about identity. It reveals the wrong reactions that come when we forget who we are, as well as the godly responses that come with remembering. Adam and Eve listened to the Serpent, bought into his lies, and ate the forbidden fruit because they forgot their true identity—the identity God gave them! They were not independent decision makers. They were God's creatures, intended to live within the boundaries God had designed for them.

As the Bible's story continues, the results of such forgetting are repeated again and again. Sarah and Abraham plotted to fulfill God's promise to them their own way instead of trusting God. If you are embracing your identity as a child of God and, therefore, an inheritor of his promises, you can rest as you wait for him to keep his promise in his wise time. The children of Israel forgot their identity as the children of the Lord Almighty, the King and Ruler of the universe. So they feared the surrounding nations instead of God, married their daughters, and worshiped their idols. King Saul forgot his true identity as an earthly king representing the one true heavenly King when he kept the plunder of holy war for himself instead of offering it to God. The disciples forgot that they were the chosen stewards of the Messiah's kingdom work, so they hid in fear as the Messiah faced death. Peter forgot his identity as the gospel messenger for all the nations and gave in to the pressure of Jewish Christians, rejecting his Gentile brothers.

However, there are also many examples of people who did remember their identity. Moses led the children of Israel through the Red Sea, with walls of water on either side, because he remembered who he was, the chosen leader of God's people with God's power as his resource. David walked boldly toward Goliath. Shadrach, Meshach, and Abednego refused to worship Nebuchadnezzar's golden image, even though they risked being burned to death. They remembered who they were and were not afraid of the king's threats. Paul and Silas sang hymns in the Philippian jail. You can only do that if you have remembered that your welfare and freedom are in the hands of an all-powerful God who is your Father. Much of the drama of God's people is a drama of identity.

What does this have to do with relationships? Everything! Although these examples are not all about relationships, they argue a very important point. Who you tell yourself you are has a very powerful impact on the way you deal with the big and small issues of daily life. In the same way, where you find your identity will have everything to do with how you respond to the hard work of relationships with others. Either I get my identity vertically, out of my sense of who God is and who he has made me in Christ, or I will seek to get my identity horizontally, out of my circumstances, relationships, and successes.

Rob was getting his identity from the success of his business; this shaped the way he looked at everything Matt did. Matt, meanwhile, was getting his identity from Rob's approval and appreciation, which altered the way he heard everything Rob had to say. Rob walked around with low-grade irritation because he took it personally whenever Matt disagreed with his business plans. Matt, meanwhile, felt like there was nothing he could ever do to win Rob's respect.

When we live out of a sense of who we are *in* Christ, we live our lives based on all we have been given *by* Christ. This keeps us from seeking to get those things from the people and situations around us. This is why there are so many identity statements in the New Testament. (Here are a few: Ephesians 1–3; Colossians 1:21–23; Hebrews 10:19–25; 1 Peter 2:9–12; 1 John 3:1–3.) Much of the disappointment and heartache we experience is the result of our attempts to get something from relationships that we already have in Christ. In almost thirty years of counseling, I have talked with countless women in difficult marriages who said, "All I ever wanted was for my husband to make me happy." My first thought is invariably, *Well, then, he's cooked!*

No human being was ever meant to be the source of personal joy and contentment for someone else. And surely, no sinner is ever going to be able to pull that off day after day in the all encompassing relationship of marriage! Your spouse, your friends, and your children cannot be the sources of your identity. When you seek to define who you are through those relationships, you are actually asking another sinner to be your personal messiah, to give you the inward rest of soul that only God can give. Only when I have sought my identity in the proper place (in my relationship with God) am I able to put you in the proper place as well. When I relate to you knowing that I am God's child and the recipient of his grace, I am able to serve and love you. I have the hope and courage to get my hands dirty with the hard work involved when two sinners live together. And you are able to do the same with me!

However, if I am seeking to get identity *from* you, I will watch you too closely, listen to you too intently, and need you too fundamentally. I will ride the roller coaster of your best and worst moments and everything in between. And because I am watching you too closely, I will become acutely aware of your weaknesses and failures. I will become overly critical, frustrated, disappointed, hopeless, and angry. I will be angry not because you are a sinner, but because you have failed to deliver the one thing I seek from you: identity. But none of us will ever get the well-being that comes from knowing who we are from our relationships. Instead, we will be left with damaged relationships filled with hurt, frustration, and anger. Matt and Rob had reached that point. They dreaded going to work and talking to each other. They both felt personally wounded by things that simply were not as personal as they believed them to be. Why? Because they were trying to find their identities in things that were never meant to provide them.

When I remember that Christ has given me everything I need to be the person he has designed me to be, I am free to serve and love you. When I know who I am, I am free to be humble, gentle, patient, forbearing, and loving as we navigate the inevitable messiness of relationships. *Is there evidence that you are looking to your relationships to give you things you have already been given in Christ?*

Remembering Who God Is

Worship is another issue that is inextricably bound up with who we are as human beings. Don't let the word *worship* trip you up here. We are not simply talking about the formal religious activities that go on at church. Worship is first an *identity* before it becomes an *activity*. That is, you and I *are* worshipers, which is why we worship. Our hearts are always under the control of something, and whatever controls your heart will control your behavior. As Bob Dylan so pointedly wrote, "You gotta serve somebody."

In Matthew 6, Christ explains that whatever we worship will become the thing that controls us. He uses a wonderful word to explain the connection: "treasure." A treasure is something with *assigned* value. That is why the saying goes, "One man's trash is another man's treasure." In Matthew 6:19–24, Christ reminds us that we all live for some kind of treasure. What we decide is valuable is what will control our hearts (v. 21). If you pay attention to yourself, this is easy to see. When you get what you think is valuable, you are happy and encouraged; when you don't, you are sad and frustrated. Finally, Christ says that what controls our hearts controls our behavior (v. 24). If something is valuable to us, we will seek to get it through the situations and relationships of daily life.

This has many implications for relationships, because only when I am worshiping God for who he is am I able to love you as you are. Real love and esteem for other people are always rooted in our worship of God. Are you struggling to see how the two are linked? Here are three ways to make the connection.

To love you as I should, I must worship God as Creator

I must look at you with the eyes of David in Psalm 139:

> For God created your inmost being;
>> he knit you together in your mother's womb.
> I praise God because you are fearfully and
>> wonderfully made;
>> his works are wonderful,
>> I know that full well.
> Your frame was not hidden from God

when you were made in the secret place.
When you were woven together in the depths
of the earth,
his eyes saw your unformed body.
(Psalm 139:13–16a, authors' adaptation)

What beautiful, amazing, and important words! If I do not see the wise work of the Creator when I look at you, it will affect the way I relate to you. God wants me to remember that his hands formed every part of you. His attention never wandered, his hand never slipped, he made no mistakes, and there were no accidents. The shape of your chin, the size of your frame, your personality, your intellectual gifts, your natural abilities, the color of your hair and skin, the timbre of your voice, the way you walk, and a million other things that make you who you are were all crafted by a gloriously wise Creator. You are the creature you are because of his beautiful plan.

Although most of us have affirmed that God is the Creator of all things, it is quite easy to worship him as Creator on Sunday and curse his work during the week. We do this when we are dissatisfied with the way God has made the people we relate to every day. When we fail to worship God as Creator in our relationships, we try to ascend to his throne and do all we can to recreate others in our *own* image. This always leads to frustration and failure.

Do you secretly wish that your boyfriend was a little more physically attractive? Do you get frustrated because your friend is not as intellectual as you are? Are you doing all you can to make that mechanical person more relational? Do you wish your shy wife could learn to be the life of the party? Are you trying to turn that well-organized planner into a more spontaneous person? Have you tried your best to turn that bookworm into an athlete like yourself? Are you frustrated because someone near you has no head for details, or can live with clutter, or is too much of an extrovert, or is way too silly for your liking? Does it bother you that your husband has gotten bald so young or that your wife is prematurely gray? Do you get frustrated because you are so completely different from someone close to you?

Be honest: have you ever tried to recreate someone in your own likeness? Without realizing it, that is exactly what Rob and Matt were attempting to do to each other. Rob was a visionary who was trying to turn his detail-oriented partner into a dreamer. Matt was an administrator who was trying recreate Rob into his own image (for the sake of the company, of course!). It's pretty predictable: If I am not affirming the glory of God in the way he made you (including the ways you are different from me), I will be frustrated with who you are and tempted to remake you in some way. Shawna constantly read to Mike. It drove him crazy! She was convinced that if she read to him enough, he would get excited by books and become the reader she had always wanted him to be. Her unwillingness to worship God as Mike's Creator led to all kinds of conflict.

If I am ever going to value who you are and benefit from our differences, I must look at you and see the wisdom of the Creator. But there is more.

If I am going to love you as I should, I must worship God as Sovereign

The words of Paul in Acts 17 are helpful here:

> From one man God made every nation of men, that they should inhabit the whole earth; and he determined the times set for them and the exact places where they should live. (Acts 17:26, authors' adaptation)

We all know that our lives have not gone according to our plans. We all know that we haven't written our own stories. Paul says this is because our story has been written by another. God has specifically and personally determined the details of each of our lives. That is why my story is different from yours. God determined exactly where each of us would be born, the parents who would raise us, and the culture in which we would live. When I look at you, I need to see God's sovereign hand writing your story perfectly. The person you are and the responses you make to life have been shaped by his sovereign choices and your responses to the story he has written for you. He determined that you would be part of the customs and culture of a certain ethnic group. He planned that you would be shaped by living in a certain geographical setting. He determined that you would live in a particular family, with all of its powerfully influential values and rules, spoken and unspoken. What is more, he determined that you would be involved in relationships and situations outside your home that would also have a powerful influence on everything you do. What is a relationship? The intersection of the stories of two people. The problem is that an awful lot of carnage takes place at this intersection.

If I fail to honor God's sovereignty in the influences he has placed in your life and the way those influences have shaped you, I will attempt to take God's place and clone you into my image. I will tend to think my way is better than your way, my culture better than your culture, and my customs and manners more appropriate than yours. I will be constantly frustrated by you and even more frustrated by my attempts to remake you into my image. Rob, for example, wished that Matt had grown up in a family where people got excited about the big picture. Matt, in turn, wished that Rob had not been raised by hippies who never cared much for the details of life!

In our relationships too, much of the bad communication, needless conflict, and constant frustration stem from our responses to the ways the other person is different from us. Some value community; others, privacy. Some hoard money, while others think it was meant to be spent. Some are used to a sit-down family dinner; others think a sandwich on the run is fine. We simply are not the same because God decided to write different stories for us. And he has placed us next to one another because that is exactly where he knew we needed to be for our good and for the fulfillment of his loving purposes on earth. *Are you frustrated with someone in your life? Have you been trying to reshape her to fit into your personal preferences?*

To love you as I should, I must worship God as Savior

Worshiping God as Savior means that I acknowledge that I am a sinner in relationship with other sinners. I remember that you are still in the middle of God's work of redemption—as am I. He is still convicting you, teaching you, and changing your heart. He is faithfully doing all these things at the best time and in the best way possible. None of us ever gets to be in relationship with a finished person. God's redemptive work of change is ongoing in all our lives. When I forget this, I become self-righteous, impatient, critical, and judgmental. I give in to the temptation to play God and try to change you in ways only God can. Rob and Matt were simply finding it hard to work alongside someone who wasn't perfect and therefore in need of God's work of change. Matt, for example, didn't want to keep working with someone who didn't know how to treat a business partner with respect. But God intended the arrangement to help them both grow.

When I fail to worship God as Savior, I am too casual about my sin and too focused on yours. Our relationships are often harmed when we try to atone for our own sins while condemning the other person for his. When you are sinned against, you will be impacted by the weaknesses and failures of that other person. When this happens, you need to allow God to use you as an instrument in his redemptive hands, rather than seeking to make changes in the other person yourself. Only God can accomplish these things. *Are you trying to do work in someone's life that only the Savior can do?*

The Bottom Line

Good relationships are rooted in identity and worship. Only when I remember who I am and worship God for who he is can I respond to you with patient, gentle, hopeful, and courageous love. As Matt and Rob began to see their identities correctly and began to trust God for what he alone could do, their relationship began to move in a positive direction. Rob didn't take it so personally when Matt disagreed with his plans for the business. Matt was less likely to get despondent when Rob didn't communicate respect. Because of the heart changes God was working in each of them, they were able to plan and work together better. They continued to deal with the same issues, but they now could resolve them in ways that were less adversarial and more productive.

7

Talk

If you keep on biting and devouring each other, watch out or
you will be destroyed by each other.

Galatians 5:1

He knelt down and put his arm around his little daughter, speaking
tender words of comfort. Their dog had just ripped the arm off
her favorite teddy bear. He told her how much he loved her and how
easy it would be for Mommy to sew Teddy back together again. She
wiped her eyes and, as she ran off, her smile was returning.

As they sat in my office, the anger between them was palpable. It had
been a long time since they had been able to muster a civil word for
each other. Everything they said now was laced with sarcasm and
fueled by bitterness. They used words like gunslingers and they each
had developed a very good aim. It hurt me to hear the ugly things
they said so easily. It hit me that it hadn't always been this way. There
had been a time when they had said the most loving, comforting,
and encouraging things to each other, a time when they found joy in
blessing each other with words. But those days were gone. This was
war and the guns were blazing.

As everyone laughed at the story Jim had just told about his wife, I could see a pained look on her face. I had heard him do this before. Jim was a natural storyteller and he loved entertaining a crowd, but he didn't ever tell funny stories about himself. Liz was always the punch line, and it was clear she did not enjoy the role. But Jim was far more focused on being the life of the party than he was on the pain he was causing his wife. He was too caught up in the "fun" of the moment.

Their friendship was amazing. They were able to say the toughest things to each other, things that are hard both to say and to hear, yet they could say them with love. They seemed to avoid self-serving flattery and unloving criticism. They didn't trim the truth with one another yet said what needed to be said in the best possible way. I was impressed by their enormous respect for each other, how easily their communication flowed, and how readily each seemed to listen to the other.

He seemed to look for every possible opening to disagree, criticize, or mock. If he was not silent, he was using words to hurt. Though still a teenager, his anger turned his words into a raging fire that burned everything in its path. He knew that words could hurt, and he used that power to his advantage. He argued every point, pointed out every weakness, mocked everyone, and made more threats than he could ever make good on. His parents and siblings avoided talking to him. It was just too exhausting and hurtful.

It was a hot summer evening in the Pennsylvania mountains. He sat with eight squirming little boys and unfolded the mysteries of God's grace to them with his Bible in hand. His words were well-chosen and clear. He seemed to know that what he would say that night had the power to change their lives forever. He never got impatient when they fidgeted; he never got sidetracked. His words rang with authority, but not because he yelled or lectured. His words had the authority of grace; he seemed to know that was enough. I was one of those boys and my life was forever changed by the words he spoke that night.

What Is It about Words?

Whenever I talk about talk, I get frustrated. All the words we use to describe communication seem too utilitarian. "We had a *talk*." "I gave her the *word*." "He gave me another *speech*." "We just can't *communicate*." "It was a long *discussion*." "We took time to *share* with one another." "There isn't enough *back and forth* in our relationship." The words just don't seem to carry enough freight. They seem too ordinary. Perhaps this is because we think communication *is* ordinary. Because our communication largely takes place in the inconsequential moments of everyday life, it is easy to underestimate its significance. The moments are rare when what you say will literally be life changing. What sets the course of a person's life are the ways he responds to the little moments. The character developed in a thousand little moments is what you carry into the big, important moments.

Your everyday communication influences the shape, quality, and direction of your relationships. Every day your words give your relationships their tone. Every day you tell people what you think of them, what you want from them, and what you would like to enjoy with them. But you don't do this in grand moments of oratory. You do it in quick side comments in the bedroom as you get ready for work, or at the curb as you hop into your car, or in the kitchen as you grab a sandwich, or over dessert at the local bistro, or in the family room during a commercial.

Because our talk lives in the world of the ordinary, it is easy to forget its true significance. It is easy to forget the impact our words have on every relationship. There has never been a good relationship without good communication. And there has never been a bad relationship that didn't get that way in part because of something that was said. Our ability to express ourselves verbally is anything but ordinary. It gets right to the heart of who God made us as our Creator, and how he is remaking us as our Savior.

In this chapter we invite you to listen to your words and evaluate the way they shape your relationships. More than that, we invite you to look at your words through the lens of Scripture. The Bible has much to say about our world of talk. The Bible does not consider this area of life ordinary and unimportant. In fact, it does the opposite. It assigns words the extraordinary value they actually deserve. This chapter invites you to consider the life-changing help you can find in the person and promises of the Lord Jesus Christ for your struggle with words.

God's Perspective on Our Words

What help does the Bible offer about words, anyway? Perhaps you're thinking, *All I know is that I wouldn't want to listen to a recording of everything I said in the last month. It would be very embarrassing!* Or, *I'm in a marriage where it seems like we just don't talk. When we try, it gets ugly really quickly.* Or perhaps, *I just don't know what to say to my friend when she unburdens her heart; I'm always fumbling for words.* Or maybe, *I'm not happy with the way I talk to my children. I try to say the right thing, but I always end up blowing it.*

The good news is that the Bible speaks practically into each of these experiences. The Bible can help you diagnose where you are in your talk and how to get where you need to be. Here's a look at words through the lens of Scripture.

Our words have power

There is an amazing proverb that Eugene Peterson translates like this: "Words kill, words give life; they're either poison or fruit—you choose."[1] This illustrates the constructive and destructive power of words while alerting us to the fact that our words always have direction. They are going either toward life or toward death. The most destructive thing words could produce is death, so the phrase "words kill" is intended to summarize all the angry, hurtful, slanderous, selfish, bitter, divisive, and demeaning forms of talk. The phrase "words give life" summarizes all the encouraging, comforting, peaceful, upbuilding, grateful, unifying, and loving forms of communication. Because our words have power and direction, they always produce some kind of harvest. It will be a life harvest of comfort, encouragement, hope, insight, unity, and joy, or a death harvest of fear, discouragement, falsehood, division, and

1   Eugene Peterson, The Message (Colorado Springs, CO: NavPress, 2002), Proverbs 18:21.

sadness. Words can open up the mysteries of the universe for someone. Words can crush a person's spirit, excite, anger, or stimulate love. Words have power.

Our words belong to the Lord

It may seem too obvious to say, but Genesis 1 makes it plain that the first words ever spoken were spoken by God. Language is not a human invention to be used in whatever way serves our interests. If God is the first speaker, then language is his creation. This means that our ability to speak was given to us by the Creator and it exists for his glory. Everything we will ever say belongs to him and should be used for his purposes. Words, in short, have a high and holy calling. Words separate you from the rest of creation, making you more like God than like animals. The gift of words calls us to live and speak in a God-focused manner. One of our greatest mistakes in communication is to take words as our own to use as we please. This is what the teenager does as he publicly mocks a friend. This is what the husband does as he criticizes his wife at dinner. This is what friends do as they gossip on the phone. This is what the demanding, critical parent does. They are all stealing God's glory by treating words as their own creation.

The world of talk is a world of trouble

Nobody articulates this more powerfully than James: "If anyone is never at fault in what he says, he is a perfect man, able to keep his whole body in check" (James 3:2b). Who can honestly say that all his words are well-intentioned and appropriately spoken? Who has not hurt someone with words or used words for a selfish purpose? Who hasn't used words as a weapon of anger rather than an instrument of peace? Don't let yourself back away from the troubles. If you are honest, you have to admit that your relationships have been troubled by words as much as they have been helped. James calls us to admit that our words are the most powerful and consistent indicators of our need for the grace of Christ. James says that if we were without fault in this area, we would be perfect in every way. So listen to your words. Don't they expose how deep your need is for God's forgiving grace? We stain our relationships with thoughtless and evil words. We are guilty of turning this gift into a weapon. We need forgiveness and we need help.

Word problems are heart problems

Christ said, "The good man brings good things out of the good stored up in his heart, and the evil man brings evil things out of the evil stored up in his heart. *For out of the overflow of his heart his mouth speaks*" (Luke 6:45, authors' emphasis). Our problem with words is not primarily a matter of vocabulary, skill, or timing. Have you ever said, "Oops, I didn't mean to say that!" Often it would be more accurate to say, "I'm sorry I said what I meant!" If the thought, attitude, desire, emotion, or purpose hadn't been in your heart, it wouldn't have come out of your mouth. Christ isn't saying that people never put their feet in their mouth and say something stupid. We all have. But he is asking us to own the connection between our thoughts, desires, and words. The real problem with your communication is *what* you want to say and *why* you want to say it, which ultimately has nothing to do with your language skills. Christ reveals that the *what* and the *why* are shaped by the heart. Therefore, if we hope to transform the way we talk with one another, the heart must change first.

A Radical Commitment to the Call of Christ

God has an agenda for our relationships. For that reason, proper communication is not so much about getting what we want out of our relationships as it is being part of what God is seeking to do. Paul captures this powerfully in 2 Corinthians 5:20: "We are therefore Christ's *ambassadors*, as though God were making his appeal through us. We implore you on Christ's behalf: Be reconciled to God" (authors' emphasis). An ambassador does one thing only—represent. His job is to incarnate a king who is not present. Every word he speaks is directed by the king's interests and will. This is exactly what God is calling us to do. What we say must be driven by what God is seeking to accomplish in us and in the other person.

What is he seeking to accomplish? Paul captures that with one word too: *reconciliation*. God's intent is that we would "no longer live for ourselves, but for him who died for us and was raised again" (2 Corinthians 5:15, authors' adaptation). God is working in every situation and relationship to reclaim our wandering hearts. He wants to make us people who are more interested in what he wants for us than what we want for ourselves. He will not relent until we are free from our slavery to an agenda of personal happiness. And he calls us to speak in a way that has this reconciliation agenda in view.

Unfortunately, we lose sight of reconciliation in many ways: When you flatter your friend because you want her to like you. When you trim the truth to avoid a conflict. When you yell at your child about his messy room. When winning an argument is all you care about. When you indulge in gossip. When you are better at pointing out wrong than asking for forgiveness. When you use words to hurt someone rather than help him. When your communication stays resolutely impersonal. When your words make you the center of attention.

Here is the point: Your words are always in pursuit of some kind of kingdom. You are either speaking as a mini-king, seeking to establish your will in your relationships and circumstances; or you are speaking as an ambassador, seeking to be part of what the *King* is doing. There is no end to the battle of words when two mini-kings talk to each other! When our words reflect the self-focused desires of our hearts rather than God's work of reconciliation, there is no end to our struggle. When we use words to establish our will rather than submit to God's, we plunge into difficulty. If we are ever going to be helped, this is where we must start.

This is why James says that our words clearly demonstrate our need for God's grace. As sinners we want what we want when we want it, and we often see others as obstacles. We treat words as if they belong to us, to be used to get what we want. When we face how powerful our self-interest is, we are confronted by the truth that only a change in our hearts can produce a change in our words.

Talking Like an Ambassador

What does it mean to communicate like an ambassador? Does it mean that you quote Scripture incessantly or constantly point out the sin in others? Does it mean I can never talk about sports or the weather? What about the daily need to discuss the details of schedules, responsibilities, problems, and plans with the people I live with? Again, the apostle Paul helps us in Ephesians 4:29–30:

> Do not let any unwholesome talk come out of your mouths,
> but only what is helpful for building others up according to

their needs, that it may benefit those who listen. And do not grieve the Holy Spirit of God, with whom you were sealed for the day of redemption.

Here is a wonderfully practical model of ambassadorial communication. Speaking as an ambassador is not about using biblical words; it's about speaking with a biblical agenda. If you want your words to reflect what God wants more than what you want, you should consider three things:

Consider the person ("only what is helpful for building others up")

Wholesome communication is other-centered communication. When my words are shaped more by my interests than yours, they lose their shelter from difficulty. Paul says I should never say anything to you that is not helpful for you. Since God is focused on remaking you into his image, I should speak in a way that builds you up. This is not just a matter of what I say, but how I say it. I now have a redemptive agenda for talking about everything. I want all of our talk to be redemptively constructive, from the most mundane details to the huge life decisions. I never want my words to be an obstacle to the work God is doing. *The words of an ambassador are always other-centered.*

Consider the problem ("according to their needs")

An ambassador is always asking, "What is the problem at this moment?" Before I speak, I must think about what you are struggling with and what you most need. Do you need encouragement, comfort, hope, direction, wisdom, courage, rebuke, warning, forgiveness, patience, teaching, correction, thanks, insight, a job description, or something else? My words must be shaped by your need. *An ambassador's words always address the person's true need of the moment.*

Consider the process ("that it may benefit those who listen")

This means that I focus on the best way to say what needs to be said. Ambassadorial communication is not just about the content of our words, but the manner in which they are spoken. Often we choose to say the right thing in the wrong way or at the wrong time. But the communication process, as much as the content of the words, needs to benefit the person. Confronting a teenager five minutes before she leaves for school is not helpful, even if the content is accurate. Rebuking a friend for an offense in front of others is not helpful. Asking your husband to consider how you hurt him as he is trying to get to sleep is not helpful. *An ambassador seeks to speak the right thing in the best way.*

Paul's practical model to guide our words ends with something very interesting: "Do not grieve the Holy Spirit." When you and I speak as mini-kings to get our own way, our words are unhelpful and untimely. Not only do we hurt and grieve other people, we also grieve the Lord. This kind of talk completely obstructs what he wants to do in and through us in our relationships. Here is where we all must remember that our relationships have been designed as workrooms for redemption, not shelters for human happiness. If we are ever going to give grace when we talk, we need grace to free us from our bondage to ourselves so that our words may be liberated to be used by God.

8

Obstacles

Do not be overcome by evil, but overcome evil with good.
Romans 12:21

On the one hand we must never imagine that our own unaided efforts can be relied on to carry us even through the next twenty-four hours as "decent" people. If He does not support us, not one of us is safe from some gross sin. On the other hand, no possible degree of holiness or heroism which has ever been recorded on the greatest saints is beyond what He is determined to produce in every one of us in the end. The job will not be completed in this life: but He means to get us as far as possible before death.[1]

Conflict with others is one of God's mysterious, counterintuitive ways of rescuing us from ourselves. God uses it to get us where he wants to take us before we die. Because we don't usually think that trials can be used in such a positive way, this truth catches us by surprise. But it shouldn't. All kinds of suffering, including conflict with others, can be redemptive because of the grace of God. By redemptive, we mean that God can use conflict (as well as everything else in our lives) to defeat sin in us and make us more like Christ, with a love for him and others that reflects his nature.

---

1   C. S. Lewis, *Mere Christianity* (New York: Macmillan, 1943), 173–174.

Conflicting Agendas

The option before Ashley seemed obvious, even biblical. Her friend had just hurt her and she was angry, but the whole thing had been brewing for years. Competition had slowly infected the friendship. Ashley hated the way things had been going and she just wanted it to end. Now it was time for her to speak her mind!

For the better part of five years, Ashley and Hannah had worked side by side in campus ministry. They loved what they did and they loved doing it together. But Hannah had been slowly seeking to undermine Ashley's relationship with the students. She wanted to be seen as the one who was more capable and in charge. To put it bluntly, she wanted the students to like and admire her more than Ashley. Now Ashley felt as if things had gotten out of control, so she made an appointment to meet with Hannah.

Ashley began the meeting by accusing Hannah of talking about her negatively to some students. "I can't believe you talk that way behind my back! I have never done that to you and I never would." Ashley's hurt had boiled over into anger and accusation. Hannah denied everything. "I can't believe you would accuse me of saying those things to other people. I thought our friendship was stronger than that. How come you have held this in for five years? Why didn't you just come to me earlier?"

As the two talked, the origin of the problem began to emerge. While talking to someone who did not care for Ashley, Hannah had made a casual comment about how "task-oriented" Ashley could be. She said it was a real pain to live with her at times. This remark took on a life of its own when the other person repeated it to others, with her own embellishments. Eventually the word found its way back to Ashley. By then it sounded as if Hannah saw her as a task-oriented demon who just used people to accomplish her ministry goals.

This little conflict was no tempest in a teapot. Ashley and Hannah had significant agendas that caused a collision in their friendship. Hannah had insinuated that Ashley's controlling ways were not just an aspect of her temperament, but a sin. Granted, her comment was subtle, but it was premeditated and calculated to make Ashley look bad to this particular student. Hannah was seeking to say, "I am better than Ashley and you should admire me more."

Facing Conflict Head On

It's inevitable. If you live with other sinners, you will have conflict. The closer you are to someone, the more potential there is for conflict. Relationships are costly, but so is avoiding them. If you choose to avoid them, you will minimize the conflict in your life, but that safety has liabilities of its own. If you choose to face conflict head on, it is full of risks and the potential for great hurt, but it can also be redemptive. Either way, you will not remain untouched by your decision. What is your tendency? Do you tend to avoid conflict? Do you rush into it? Or do you move into conflict with a God-centered perspective?

If what we have been saying in this book is true, there are right and wrong choices here. And if what we have been saying about the triune God is true, you must move toward people, not away from them. Remember, Father, Son, and Spirit were torn apart when Jesus died so that we might embrace rather than exclude one another. We have to be willing to face conflict. God wants us to grow and this is a crucial place where growth often occurs. He wants to make us more like Christ, and he wants to use others to make that happen. He wants Ashley and Hannah to mirror his image. He has put them together to accomplish this purpose. Undoubtedly, neither Ashley nor Hannah thinks that God has made the right choice! And if you are in the midst of conflict right now, you probably know how they feel. But it's true: God is working overtime to rescue you from yourself.

The Cause and Cure of Ungodly Conflict

Why do we fight? Why do we struggle with other people? Why can't at least one relationship in our lives come with a "no conflict" label attached to it? Some people think that is what marriage is for! These people are in for a surprise. In reality, marriage is the most likely place for conflict. But close relationships like marriage are also the most likely places for supernatural change to occur.

If you have a problem, conflict is a good one to have. Why? Because conflict is a problem the Bible addresses very directly. You don't have to be an expert Bible scholar to get help here. All you need is a heart that is ready and willing to hear the answer. One passage that diagnoses the reason for conflict and offers a cure is found in the very practical book of James.

Question 1: Why do we fight with one another?

Good question. James asks the same question. We can be thankful that he answers it as well.

> What causes fights and quarrels among you? Don't they come from your desires that battle within you? You want something but don't get it. You kill and covet, but you cannot have what you want. You quarrel and fight. You do not have, because you do not ask God. When you ask, you do not receive, because you ask with wrong motives, that you may spend what you get on your pleasures. (James 4:1–3)

Now, that's pretty concise! Notice that James is saying just the opposite of what we often say in conflict. We usually say something like, "I did that because you. . . ." or "I wouldn't be so angry if you wouldn't. . . ." Our typical response to conflict is to point the finger at our opponent. We feel justified because the person often has done something annoying, frustrating, or even downright sinful! But James doesn't let us off the hook that easily. He makes it clear that even if someone has sinned against us, the reason we fight is because there is something wrong going on inside us! He says, "Don't these fights come from your desires that battle within you? You want something but you don't get it." The word "desire" that James uses here is a word that would better be translated as "selfish desire." All desires are not wrong. But a selfish desire is.

Conflict broke out between me and my wife the other day in our kitchen. I was putting dishes in the dishwasher and she was cooking dinner. We both got in each other's way and then got sarcastic with each other. I said, "I would hate to get in your way while I load the dishwasher!" She replied, "I would hate to get in your way while I cook dinner!" What was going on? I had a desire to accomplish a task and was feeling rather self-righteous about what a sacrificial husband I was. My wife also had a desire to accomplish a task and was feeling self-righteous about what a sacrificial wife and mother she was. Both of our desires, on the surface, were good desires: I wanted to help in the kitchen and she wanted to serve the family by cooking dinner. But these desires quickly turned from good to selfish. I wanted to serve, but it had to be on my terms and on my time schedule. My wife wanted to serve, but she wanted to do it without any distractions. The selfishness showed itself in our self-righteous comments. We both wanted to be recognized for our service, and when that did not happen we had conflict. We divorced our service from God's glory and the other's good and turned it into self-service: "I'll serve when I want to and I want to be appreciated when I do."

What tends to produce conflict in your life? Is it comfort, pleasure, recognition, power, control, or acceptance? Here's how those good things can become "selfish desires" that lead to conflict. (Notice, too, that the opposite of what we want is what we fear.) *These things are not sinful in and of themselves until they turn selfish.* Comfort, pleasure, recognition, power, control, or acceptance can be blessings to be enjoyed. But they become sinful when we allow them to move from blessings to things that replace the One who blesses. Consider how the following good things morph into something sinful:

- **Comfort.** I want, must have, and deserve comfort and you'd better not get in the way of me getting it! I fear hard work.
- **Pleasure.** I want, must have, and deserve pleasure and you'd better give it to me! I fear pain.
- **Recognition.** I want, must have, and deserve recognition or I will be devastated. I fear being overlooked.
- **Power.** I want, must have, and deserve power and you'd better do what I say! I fear being told what to do.
- **Control.** I want, must have, and deserve control and you will feel the brunt of my disappointment if you mess up my tidy little universe! I fear unpredictability.
- **Acceptance.** I want, must have, and deserve acceptance and you are responsible to give it to me. I fear rejection.

Can you identify with any of these? Maybe you could add something to this list. Think of the last time you were in conflict with another person. What desire turned ugly as it became self-centered? James says that these are the kinds of things that bubble under the surface of conflict. Both Ashley and Hannah are struggling at this level. What is the real problem in their relationship?

Perhaps you would say that Hannah should not have spoken negatively about Ashley to someone else. You could also say that

Ashley confronted Hannah in an ungodly way when her reputation was tarnished. Both statements are true, yet the problems in their relationship go deeper. For Ashley, her reputation mattered more to her than anything else. For Hannah, what mattered most was recognition in ministry. Neither desire is bad in and of itself, but Hannah and Ashley had allowed them to become things they wanted more than God or the other's good. A good reputation and recognition can be good things, but not when they are life-dominating and all-consuming. As soon as they are divorced from God's glory and the needs of others, they become self-glorifying and self-serving. In other words, God's glory and love of neighbor have been replaced with self-glory and self-love. Do you see how things have gotten turned upside down?

Question 2: What has become more important to me than my relationship with God?

James asks us this question because he wants us to see how serious it is to make something like comfort, pleasure, power, control, acceptance, or recognition a selfish desire. If you don't recognize this, you won't grow in your ability to handle conflict in a redemptive way.

> You adulterous people, don't you know that friendship with
> the world is hatred toward God? Anyone who chooses to be
> a friend of the world becomes an enemy of God. (James 4:4)

When we make something other than God first in our lives, James says we have become too friendly with the world and committed spiritual adultery. This is no small matter. Ashley and Hannah, who are growing Christians, have made reputation and recognition more important than God's glory and grace. God alone deserves their allegiance and attention because he alone is God. But they have made a piece of creation their best friend and primary focus. They have fallen in love with something besides God.

Do you see how this verse is both scathing and encouraging? As James says we are guilty of adultery, he uses two metaphors to describe the relationship we have with God. The image of adultery means we are married to God. When he says we are guilty of friendship with the world, he implies that God is our only rightful friend. For anyone who knows the Bible, this is wonderfully shocking! An absolutely holy God, who will not and cannot tolerate sin, has made us his bride and friend through Jesus's life, death, and resurrection!

Do you see how good and innocent things can become more important to us than God? When I was loading the dishwasher, I went from serving someone else to serving myself. I was seeking self-glory and was guilty of self-love. What innocent and good things do you live for more than God? Think of the last time you experienced ungodly irritation with a friend, spouse, coworker, or child. Ask yourself, *What was more important to me than God's glory?* What temporal blessing did you want that you did not get? What did you fear would happen if you didn't get what you wanted? These are good questions to ask as you learn to engage in conflict in godly ways.

Question 3: What does God do with people who forsake him for something else?

Consider a married couple where one of the partners has a one-night stand. This person has betrayed the one to whom he is supposed to be most committed. He has shared with another an intimacy that only the spouse can rightly claim. What would you expect the offended spouse to do? Would you expect that person to act as though nothing had happened? What if the offended spouse said, "Oh, that's okay"? Wouldn't you wonder if that person really cared about the marriage? If the offended spouse was even slightly invested in the marriage, you would expect to see some jealousy and anger over infidelity, wouldn't you?

So it is with God. God is not indifferent when we are unfaithful to him. He is a jealous God who cares deeply about his relationship with us. Even when we stray and find ourselves in the arms of false lovers, he is roused to act on our behalf. God pursues us for our good, as we see in these startling verses:

> Or do you think Scripture says without reason that the spirit he caused to live in us envies intensely? But he gives us more grace. That is why Scripture says: "God opposes the proud but gives grace to the humble." (James 4:5–6)

These verses are somewhat hard to decipher, but here is the gist of what God does when we stray. When we wander from God, the Spirit he has poured out on us and who now lives in us becomes very concerned and jealous. A better way to translate the word "jealous" is "zealous." The word "jealousy" has negative connotations, but it can actually be a very positive word. Like the person whose spouse has been unfaithful, God is zealous to do whatever it takes to regain the affection of our hearts. He doesn't do this because he needs us; he does it because he loves us. When he pursues us and we humble ourselves and return to him, he then pours out even more grace!

What do you think God typically uses to regain our affection? Ironically, he uses other people! That is one of the blessings of conflict. He uses the difficult seasons in our relationships to allow us to see what we typically live for besides him. Take the small spat my wife and I had in the kitchen. The only way I would see that I sometimes serve others obstacles out of self-glory and self-love was to put my wife next to me in the kitchen. The only way for my wife to see her own sinful tendencies was to put me in the kitchen with her! This is true of all of our relationships. God uses other people to mysteriously and counterintuitively rescue us from self-glory and self-love. Why does he do that? Because he loves us more than we love ourselves!

Consider Hannah and Ashley. Both of these women were maturing Christians and yet they struggled with each other at a fundamental level. Without Ashley, Hannah would not be able to see that she often lives to be recognized for her Christian service. The same is true for Ashley. God loves them both, so he put them together so that they could see themselves and grow in repentance and faith. Who is God using in your life this way? Do you see that your wise, sovereign, and gracious Redeemer is acting on your behalf when he placed this person in your life? If so, you are growing in your ability to engage in conflict in godly ways. Remember, you can't avoid conflict, but it can be a place where amazing growth takes place!

Question 4: Once we are rescued, what should we do?

The answer to this question is found in James 4:7–10. Seeing God's redeeming love should lead us to grow in the joy of daily repentance and faith. Seeing, admitting, confessing, and forsaking sin (repentance), in combination with seeing, acknowledging, and adoring Christ (faith), is the only dynamic that can change a warmaker into a peacemaker. These verses combine the sobering reality of our sin with the life-changing promises of grace:

> Submit yourselves, then, to God. Resist the devil, and he will flee from you. Come near to God and he will come near to you. Wash your hands, you sinners, and purify your hearts, you double-minded. Grieve, mourn and wail. Change your laughter to mourning and your joy to gloom. Humble yourselves before the Lord, and he will lift you up. (James 4:7–10)

James calls the person in conflict to engage in spiritual warfare. The devil uses parts of creation to entice your still-sinful heart away from God. He wants you to fall prey to self-glory and self-love. James has already said that you are receiving grace so that you can humble yourself. He now *commands* you to be humble and to cry out to God for help. Through this process your heart is changed, and you begin to see that your allegiance to something other than God is a serious matter. As you repent, you experience the purification of your heart, and your behavior begins to change as well. As you are laid low by God's grace, he promises to lift you up! You are being turned right-side up. You are placing your life within the bigger circle of God's glory and renewing your love for him. Conflict can now be godly, and good things begin to happen between you and other people. As C. S. Lewis says, when you put first things first, second things are increased, not decreased.

In the kitchen that night, my wife and I experienced God's grace and moved in a different direction after our disagreement. Rather than continuing to point the finger and fight for our own glory, self-protection, and self-love, we confessed our sin, asked for forgiveness, and continued working together. You may be wondering why I would share such a minor incident. It's because if we don't grow in these little moments, we won't grow when the harder times come. If Ashley and Hannah can't grow in their relationship, where there is a significant amount of commitment and love, how will they ever grow when they are called to love an enemy?!

Let's Get Practical

To apply what James 4 teaches, you have to begin with relationships built on commitment and love. Within those relationships you can start to form habits that can be practiced later in tougher moments of conflict. What does it look like to engage in godly conflict in the heat of the moment? Here are some suggestions:

Understand that conflict is one way God works in our lives

Conflict can be good. God himself engages in conflict. In fact, the Bible is a book about God entering into conflict in order to save us. He comes humbly, in the person of Christ, and fights on our behalf against the ravages of sin. He suffers, dies, and is raised as the victor over sin and death. He calls us to imitate him as we engage in conflict with others. Godly conflict is an act of compassion!

Identify what drives ungodly conflict in your life

What tends to lure your loyalty and affection away from God? Be specific, and don't be surprised if each instance of ungodly conflict reveals a different idol in your life. Is it acceptance, power, control, recognition, comfort, pleasure, or being right? These are among the most common idols in people's lives.

Recognize your default strategy in conflict

Most of us have a default strategy we use to get what we want. Do you love to fight because you have to be right? Do you avoid conflict because you don't want people to disapprove of you? Do you avoid conflict because you don't like discomfort?

Engage in specific and intelligent spiritual warfare

When you see what you typically live for and how you try to get it, you can start to grow in repentance and faith. You want to be brutally honest about your sin, but you also want to be ardently hopeful about what Christ has done for you on the cross. You want to remember that, because you have the Holy Spirit, you already have the resources available to fight against ungodly conflict!

Consider the other person

As your heart is reclaimed by the grace of God, ask questions about what it will look like to engage in godly conflict. Do you need to pursue someone and confront him? Do you need to be patient and encourage him? Do you need to overlook an offense? What sins and weaknesses in the other person do you need to consider as you decide what your next move will be? In 1 Thessalonians, the apostle Paul lovingly encourages the church to engage in godly conflict with one another. In verses 14–18 of chapter 5, Paul says that there are different ways to confront, based upon what the person needs and mwhat will build him up.

> And we urge you, brothers, warn those who are idle, encourage the timid, help the weak, be patient with everyone. Make sure that nobody pays back wrong for wrong, but always try to be kind to each other and to everyone else. Be joyful always; pray continually; give thanks in all circumstances, for this is God's will for you in Christ Jesus. (1 Thessalonians 5:14–18)

There are times to warn, encourage, and help the person with whom we are in conflict. We are called to always be patient and renounce revenge.[2] Verse 16 grounds this kind of lifestyle in worship. If we are not worshiping God and keeping him first in our lives, we will fail miserably and do more to harm people than to help them.

Make a plan to approach the person

If you think that patience has run its course and you need to address an issue, approach the person in this way:

Own whatever personal sin you have brought to the situation. Only do this if you have sin to own. Sometimes you will and sometimes you won't. Most of the time we do bring sin into the situation, so don't be afraid to admit where you have not loved well. Your confidence in Christ's righteousness (not your own) is the only thing that will enable you to do this!

---

2   We will say more about forgiving others in the next chapter. Asking for and offering forgiveness are critical parts of redeeming our relationships. We will make mistakes, but even then there is hope!

Name the problem. There may be more than one problem you mneed to address. Be specific so that you are both dealing with the same problem. Only deal with one problem at a time!

Explore possible solutions. Stay focused on the problem and come with a desire to deal with it. Suggest possible alternative solutions and choose one to implement.

Implement the agreed-upon solution. Be specific and determine what it will look like.

Evaluate your implementation. Make a commitment to get together again and evaluate how the solution is working. Such a commitment is a form of accountability. It communicates a deep commitment to the relationship.

If you get stuck and things don't improve, be willing to get outside help. Together you should choose a person you believe will respect both sides of the conflict.

No one ever said that conflict would be fun! But the Christian life is not always fun. That is not the most important thing to God. He is committed to something much bigger. His kingdom plan involves a total restoration of what he has made. He will settle for nothing less in his creation than to see that all things ultimately bring him glory. He will be the center of everything at the end of the age, and when that happens we will be most satisfied. Right now, he is using conflict to work out this comprehensive plan in you. Take heart, for he is present in your struggles and he is fighting on your behalf!

We started the chapter with a quote from C. S. Lewis. Let's complete it here:

> That is why we must not be surprised if we are in for a rough time. When a man turns to Christ and seems to be getting on pretty well (in the sense that some of his bad habits are now corrected), he often feels that it would now be natural if things went fairly smoothly. When troubles come along—illnesses, money troubles, new kinds of temptation—he is disappointed. These things, he feels, might have been necessary to rouse him and make him repent in his bad old days; but why now? Because God is forcing him on, or up, to a higher level: putting him in situations where he will have to be very much braver, or more patient, or more loving, than

he ever dreamed of being before. It seems to us all unnecessary: but that is because we have not yet had the slightest notion of the tremendous thing He means to make of us.

I find I must borrow yet another parable from George MacDonald. Imagine yourself as a living house. God comes in to rebuild that house. At first, perhaps, you can understand what He is doing. He is getting the drains right and stopping the leaks in the roof and so on: you knew that those jobs needed doing and so you are not surprised. But presently he starts knocking the house about in a way that hurts abominably and does not seem to make sense. What on earth is He up to? The explanation is that He is building quite a different house from the one you thought of—throwing out a new wing here, putting on an extra floor there, running up towers, making courtyards. You thought you were going to be made into a decent little cottage: but He is building a palace. He intends to come and live in it Himself.[3]

---

3   C. S. Lewis, Mere Christianity (New York: Macmillan, 1943), 174.

9

Forgiveness

You have taken from me my closest friends
and have made me repulsive to them.
I am confined and cannot escape;
my eyes are dim with grief.

Psalm 88:8–9

Grace felt betrayed, and she had been. Her husband John had met someone on the internet six months earlier; they had been having an affair for the past three. Grace found out when she used John's user name to log on to their computer. When she saw the string of Instant Messages, she was devastated. What was she going to do? She fluctuated between wanting revenge and blaming herself.

In her early teens, Heather was abused by a family member. She was in college now, living under a cloud of guilt. She kept her hair long because it covered her face; it felt like a form of protection. Like Grace, she fluctuated between revenge and guilt.

Andy and Melissa had been married for twenty years. Their marriage was strong and growing. But a few days ago, Melissa had gotten irritated when Andy came home from work late. She said something sarcastic to him—she couldn't even remember what. But Andy's response was angry, self-justifying, and critical. Days later, the tension was still there. Sin had crept up on them and created a barrier between them.

Bill loved his children and wanted them to grow up to be godly adults. They were teenagers now, developing minds of their own. One day Bill's son, Michael, came in from the backyard and slammed the door. He was upset that his brother had reneged on a promise to play basketball. Bill immediately got up and yelled at Michael for being so angry. "You have a problem, Son, and I am not going to tolerate it anymore. Your anger is out of control! Go back outside and cool down!" When Michael heard his father yell, he yelled back, turned around, and ran out the door.

Familiar Territory?

What do these vignettes have in common? Do you see yourself in any of them? The first two involve serious issues of infidelity and abuse. The latter two seem more ordinary. Each story includes people who are sinning and being sinned against. This is a given when we live in a world with other sinners.

Each scenario presents the need and opportunity to practice forgiveness. But so often in these situations, we choose to get even or pretend to ignore offenses. When we reject the opportunity to forgive or ask for forgiveness, the relationship suffers. When we choose to practice true forgiveness, the relationship is not just brought back to where it was before the offense; it actually moves further down the road to maturity. Each of these scenarios is different in degree, not in kind. In every one of them, questions arise: "How can this relationship be restored and made more meaningful?"[1] "What does it look like to practice forgiveness?" "How can I forgive without acting like what he did is okay?" "Where will I find the desire to forgive or ask for forgiveness?" "What *is* forgiveness anyway?"

No one lives a day without needing to ask these questions, and yet forgiveness is one of the most poorly practiced activities in the

---

1   This, of course, would look different when a crime is committed. In cases like Heather's, issues of forgiveness would not exclude filing criminal charges.

Christian community—if it is practiced at all. I know this from pastoral and personal experience. I had been a Christian for nearly twenty years and married for nearly ten before I understood what it meant to practice forgiveness with my wife! And yet the Bible talks about practicing forgiveness as though it were a daily thing. C. S. Lewis sums it up well:

> To forgive the incessant provocations of daily life— to keep on forgiving the bossy mother-in-law, the bullying husband, the nagging wife, the selfish daughter, the deceitful son— how can we do it? Only, I think, by remembering where we stand, by meaning our words when we say in our prayers each night, "Forgive us our trespasses as we forgive those that trespass against us." We are offered forgiveness on no other terms. To refuse it is to refuse God's mercy for ourselves. There is no hint of exceptions and God means what he says.[2]

The Lord's Prayer commands us to pray, "Forgive us our debts as we forgive our debtors," right after it instructs us to pray for daily bread. Practicing forgiveness is something we must do daily in the same way we ask for the daily provision of food. It is a part of everyday life, not something reserved for life's "big" sins and events. Let me illustrate. I have had the opportunity to meet with hundreds of couples seeking help in their marriages. One of the most common problems is the giving and receiving of forgiveness. I have met couples who have been married for twenty years, yet neither one has ever truly admitted sin and asked for forgiveness. How can this be? The Bible is a book about a God who forgives; it calls those who have been forgiven to be forgiving people. Yet so little of the forgiveness that has been received translates into forgiveness being offered. We need help! The individuals at the beginning of this chapter need help, and you need help too.

Guidance along the Path of Forgiveness

Why don't we forgive? Why isn't forgiveness practiced more in Christian churches, families, and relationships? Forgiveness is not practiced because we fail to understand what it is, but Scripture does not leave us in the dark about this vital practice. In Matthew 18:21–35,

2   C. S. Lewis, The Weight of Glory (New York: Macmillan, 1947), 125.

Jesus tells a parable. As is often the case with parables, it is powerful and unpredictable. You don't necessarily anticipate the force they will have—and you don't expect that the force will be directed at you! But Jesus's parables often sneak up and surprise us by pointing out our own failures and need for grace. This parable is no exception.

> At that point Peter got up the nerve to ask, "Master, how many times do I forgive a brother or sister who hurts me? Seven?"
>
> Jesus replied, "Seven! Hardly. Try seventy times seven.
>
> "The kingdom of God is like a king who decided to square accounts with his servants. As he got under way, one servant was brought before him who had run up a debt of a hundred thousand dollars. He couldn't pay up, so the king ordered the man, along with his wife, children, and goods, to be auctioned off at the slave market.
>
> "The poor wretch threw himself at the king's feet and begged, 'Give me a chance and I'll pay it all back.' Touched by his plea, the king let him off, erasing the debt.
>
> "The servant was no sooner out of the room when he came upon one of his fellow servants who owed him forgiveness ten dollars. He seized him by the throat and demanded, 'Pay up. Now!'
>
> "The poor wretch threw himself down and begged, 'Give me a chance and I'll pay it all back.' But he wouldn't do it. He had him arrested and put in jail until the debt was paid. When the other servants saw this going on, they were outraged and brought a detailed report to the king.
>
> "The king summoned the man and said, 'You evil servant! I forgave your entire debt when you begged me for mercy. Shouldn't you be compelled to be merciful to your fellow servant who asked for mercy?' The king was furious and put the screws to the man until he paid back his entire debt. And that's exactly what my Father in heaven is going to do to each one of you who doesn't forgive unconditionally anyone who asks for mercy."[3]

---

3   Eugene Peterson, *The Message* (Colorado Springs, CO: NavPress, 1993), Matthew 18:21–35.

This story reveals explosive truths about the nature of forgiveness, but it also gives us a glimpse of the motive that should drive our desire to forgive. As we look deeper into this parable, we will start to see what forgiveness is and why it is so important.

Forgiveness Involves Canceling a Debt

The metaphor of debt cancellation clearly defines the nature of forgiveness. The merciful king absorbed a $100,000 debt that was owed to him. When you forgive someone, you also cancel a debt. But, more specifically, you make a conscious choice to absorb the cost yourself. You choose not to make the offender pay for the offense. By forfeiting your right to collect, you make at least three promises.

You promise that you will not bring up the debt to use it as leverage. When you forgive, you are saying that you will not make the offender pay by reminding him of what he has done in an effort to control him. This does not mean that you can't discuss it and seek to deal with the offense in a redemptive way. This is where the godly conflict we discussed in the previous chapter comes into play.

You promise that you will not bring up the offense to others and slander the person who sinned against you. This does not mean that you cannot seek the advice and counsel of others as you work through the issue, but it does mean that you will not slander the person under the guise of getting outside advice. You will not gossip about what the person has done to you.

Finally, you promise not to dwell on the offense yourself. One of the biggest challenges when someone sins against you is to not replay the offense over and over again in your mind.

When you fail to forgive someone, you break these three promises. Rather than canceling the debt, you keep the person's indebtedness before him, others, and yourself. Your desire to make the person pay for what he has done outweighs your desire to forgive.

Forgiveness Is Costly, But Not Forgiving Is More Costly

No matter how you spin it, forgiveness is costly. Regardless of how big or small the offense, canceling a debt and absorbing the cost is going to hurt. But the parable shows us that not forgiving also has a price, and it is higher than the price forgiveness demands. This is where we must let the truth override our feelings since it often feels good to hold onto an offense. That good feeling, contrasted with the pain of forgiving, blinds us to the bill we're running up spiritually. Jesus clearly says that an abiding unwillingness to forgive will cost you eternally! God will treat you the same way you treat others. An entrenched refusal to forgive is a sign that you have not known God's amazing forgiveness yourself. Your ugly behavior reveals the ugly condition of your heart. In addition, holding onto an offense will make you a bitter and unloving person, and you will inevitably damage all your relationships. No matter which way you choose, you will pay a price. Which price are you willing to pay?

A failure to forgive someone will change you

Notice what the unmerciful servant does after he refuses to cancel the other servant's debt. He "seized him by the throat" (v. 28) and had him thrown into jail (v. 30)! Before the king, he was the victim of his own negligence, but his unwarranted bitterness and anger turned him into a victimizer. Do you see how easily this happens? It feels so natural to make someone pay. A sense of justice quickly goes into overdrive and turns into revenge. You may not choke anyone, but you may shut someone out of your life. Bitterness gets its foot in the door and eventually, if the situation is not addressed and forgiveness is not granted, it takes over your life. That's why it is so important to practice forgiveness on a daily basis when an offense is committed against you. If you don't start with the little skirmishes, you'll begin to lose the battles, which will eventually cost you the war.

Forgiveness is an event and a process

When Peter asks Jesus how many times he should forgive someone, he thinks he is being rather noble by suggesting seven times. But Jesus rebukes Peter and says that forgiveness has no limits. There is no way around Jesus's words, and no use trying to soften the implications. The principle applies to countless offenses and even the same, endlessly repeated offense. We're tempted to think that once we have forgiven someone, we're done. But forgiving someone is not just a past event. It's something we must continue to practice, even when we are dealing with an offense we have already forgiven. Even if I have forgiven you for something you have done in the past, I need to be careful that I don't slip into bitterness some time in the future. I need to keep practicing forgiveness every time I see you or think of you.

Why is the process of forgiveness so important? Because even if you have forgiven someone for an offense, you will be tempted to think about it the next time you see her, or the next time she sins against you. Without realizing it, you will pile that sin on top of the old sins. This makes it harder and harder to forgive someone.

Forgiveness is not forgetting

Too often people say that the evidence of having truly forgiven someone is to forget what he has done to you. The passage that is often quoted is Jeremiah 31:34, where God says, "For I will forgive their wickedness and will remember their sins no more." This verse, some say, is how we should forgive.

There are at least two problems with this understanding of forgiveness. First, it is not realistic. Our minds don't function this way, and our ability to remember is powerful. Trying to forget a sin someone has committed against you will only encourage you to remember it. It's like being told not to think about a pink elephant. What did you do the moment you read that sentence? Completely erasing an offense from your memory is not realistic. Second, it is not biblical. The passage in Jeremiah does not say that God has amnesia when he looks at you. Our omniscient God does not forget anything! The word *remember* is not a "memory" word, but a "promise" word, a covenant word. God is promising that when we confess our sins, "I will not treat you as your sins deserve. Instead, I will forgive you."

This is why forgiveness is both a past event and an ongoing process into the future. It is a past promise you keep in the future. When this is done, the memory of small offenses usually dissipates. Larger offenses probably will not. Grace will never forget about John's affair. Heather will never forget her abuse. Melissa and Andy will always be aware that they have sinned against each other. Michael will remember the times his father was sinfully angry. But each individual can still practice biblical forgiveness. They can make a promise and remain faithful to that promise over time.

It is very important to understand these two dimensions of forgiveness. If you don't, you will veer off in one of two opposite but equally wrong directions: (1) You will be plagued with doubts about whether or not you have forgiven someone because you think that forgiving equals forgetting. Or (2) you will give in to bitterness without realizing it because you think that, since you have forgiven someone in the past, you are allowed to hold onto the vestiges of hurt in the present. Grace, for example, may be plagued by doubts if she thinks that forgiving John means she should forget what he did. Or she may become subtly bitter, thinking she did all she needs to do when she granted forgiveness in the past. Neither reflects the way God has forgiven us.

Forgiveness has a vertical and a horizontal dimension

In addition to this parable, the Bible is full of calls to forgive. There are two that almost seem contradictory: Mark 11:25 and Luke 17:3. Mark 11:25 says, "And when you stand praying, if you hold anything against anyone, forgive him, so that your Father in heaven may forgive you your sins." Luke 17:3 says, "If your brother sins, rebuke him, *and if he repents*, forgive him" (authors' emphasis). Mark 11:25 seems to say that we are to forgive someone no matter what, while Luke 17:3 forgiveness seems to say that you only forgive someone if he repents. Which one of these verses is right? They're both right!

The verses are talking about two different aspects of forgiveness. Mark 11:25 is talking about forgiveness as a heart attitude before God. The context is worship. When I consider someone's sin as I stand before the Lord, I am called to have an attitude of forgiveness toward the person who sinned against me. This is non-negotiable. I do not mhave the right to withhold forgiveness and harbor bitterness in my heart. Luke 17:3, on the other hand, is talking about forgiveness as a horizontal transaction between me and the offender. This is often referred to as reconciliation. The point Luke 17:3 makes is that, while I am to have an attitude of forgiveness before the Lord, I can only grant forgiveness to the other person if he repents and admits he has sinned against me. Even if he never does this, I am called to maintain an attitude of forgiveness toward the offender. The vertical aspect of forgiveness is unconditional, but the horizontal aspect depends upon the offender admitting guilt and asking for forgiveness.

This means that Grace can say to John, "Before the Lord, I have forgiven you and I will not make you pay for what you have done." But she can only grant forgiveness to John and pursue reconciliation if he admits he has sinned and asks for her forgiveness. This is where the Bible is so realistic and nuanced. These two dimensions bring clarity to what it means to forgive. Grace may long for reconciliation between her and John. She can pave the way for reconciliation as she practices an attitude of forgiveness. But ultimately she cannot make reconciliation happen. For Grace, the vertical aspect of forgiveness is never optional, but she can't singlehandedly bring about reconciliation.

Forgiveness does not mean peace at all costs

Does it seem as if forgiveness means you should just let people sin against you? Once again, the wisdom of Scripture addresses this concern. This parable is part of a longer discussion about life in the kingdom of God. The entire chapter of Matthew 18 instructs us on how to deal with the sins of others. Matthew 18:1–5 teaches that life in the kingdom requires humility to confront someone gently about his sin. Matthew 18:6–9 teaches that life in the kingdom requires taking sin seriously. We can't sweep it under the rug in our own lives or in the lives of others. Matthew 18:10–14 teaches that life in the kingdom involves going after lost and wayward people. Real love demands pursuit. The parable we studied teaches that life in the kingdom involves radical forgiveness. And right in the middle of the chapter (vv. 15–17) you find specific instructions on how to approach someone who has sinned against you.

> "If a fellow believer hurts you, go and tell him—work it out between the two of you. If he listens, you've made a friend. If he won't listen, take one or two others along so that the presence of witnesses will keep things honest, and try again. If he still won't listen, tell the church. If he won't listen to the church, you'll have to start over from scratch, confront him with the need for repentance, and offer again God's forgiving love."[4]

4   Ibid., Matthew 18:15–17.

93

The Bible never says, "Make it easy for others to sin against you." Instead, it provides a way to deal with sin in redemptive ways. Romans 12:18 says, "If it is possible, as far as it depends on you, live at peace with everyone." Paul calls us to strive for peace, but he knows there are limits involved when you pursue someone in love. When you have reached those limits, there are other redemptive options available to you. Your attempt to love a habitually abusive, unrepentant person sometimes involves confrontation and possibly separation. Sometimes church leaders may need to be involved. Sometimes the state intervenes on the offended party's behalf.

Asking For and Granting Forgiveness

It is vital to know how to ask for and grant forgiveness. Andy and Melissa have lapsed into a bad pattern when it comes to reconciliation. When either of them sins against the other, this is what it typically sounds like: "Melissa, I'm sorry you got so upset when I yelled at you. I hate it when that happens." Melissa replies, "That's okay, Andy. I guess I was just tired after a long day at work."

If it weren't so true to life, this scene would be comical. What did Andy just do? He actually blamed the fight on Melissa! He implied that the problem was not that he yelled at her, but that she was too sensitive about it. Melissa responds by accepting the blame for Andy's sin and then excusing her own response. Early on in a relationship, these things may not seem to matter that much. But over time, this counterfeit version of seeking and granting forgiveness is deadly. No one admits any sin and no one offers or asks for forgiveness.

What should Andy and Melissa do? If there truly was a sin committed, it has to be specifically acknowledged by the person who sinned. That person then needs to ask forgiveness for the specific sin. The offended person must then choose to forgive or not. If this doesn't happen, at some point Melissa is going to become angry at Andy and say that he never admits he is wrong. Andy will likely do the same with Melissa. And they will be right!

Here's what it should sound like: "Melissa, I am sorry for yelling at you. What I did was wrong. Will you forgive me?" This time, Andy has been specific and named his sin. Melissa should not reply, "It's okay." Why? Because it is not okay for someone to sin against another person! Instead, she has a decision to make: forgive or not forgive. If she understands her own forgiveness, she will say, "Thanks for saying that. Yes, I forgive you." If she has sinned against Andy, she may even add, "Will you forgive me for being sarcastic toward you?" My wife and I have moved toward spiritual maturity as we have practiced forgiveness and communicated clearly with words that exhibit humility, honesty, and grace.

Of course, it is possible to use all the right words and not mean what you say. That's hypocrisy and has nothing to do with forgiving. When we practice forgiveness, our words flow from a humble heart that sincerely means what it says.

Apologies and Forgiveness

There is a difference between an apology and asking for forgiveness. An apology is appropriate when you have done something by accident. For example, if I accidentally spill a cup of hot coffee on you, I should say, "I am very sorry I did that." I should also do whatever I can to help you get cleaned up. But suppose I purposefully threw coffee on you because I was irritated? That is not an accident. That is a sin. I may apologize and say I am sorry, but I also need to name the sin, confess that it was wrong, and ask for forgiveness.

Forgiving by Grace

How will Grace ever forgive John? How will Heather find the strength to forgive her abuser if he repents? How will Andy and Melissa practice forgiveness in their marriage day after day? Where will Michael get the power to forgive his dad for his angry outburst? How will John get to the place where he can confess his sin and ask Grace to forgive him? If it happens, where will Heather's abuser find the strength to admit the evil he has done? Where will Melissa, Andy, and Bill get the spiritual ability to acknowledge their own sin and ask for forgiveness? What about you?

It is one thing to gain clarity on what forgiveness is and isn't; it is quite another to actually practice it. As you read this chapter, you probably thought of people who have sinned against you. You may be troubled by the call to forgive them. You may also have thought of someone you have sinned against. You know you need to ask that person to forgive you. Does this frighten you? Take heart! This passage is not just chock-full of instruction; it is also teeming with hope and promise.

The king in Jesus's parable absorbs the loss of thousands of dollars. What a generous king! Imagine if you owed $100,000 or even several million dollars in back taxes to the government. You would most likely be facing a serious prison sentence. Now, suppose a wealthy person offered to pay your debts and leave you with enough money to live like a billionaire. You would be overcome with gratitude toward this person. He would be constantly on your mind, and you would probably share this story with everyone. With your new wealth, you would likely be a very generous person, helping others who were in trouble, even those who had taken advantage of you. Not to respond in this way would raise serious questions about the condition of your soul!

Are you getting the point? The king in the parable is none other than King Jesus. He came to absorb the cost of your sin—a sin debt that makes millions of dollars look like chump change. Jesus came and shed his blood for you. The Father emptied heaven of its greatest treasure so that you could be forgiven. Read 1 Peter 1:1–9:

> I, Peter, am an apostle on assignment by Jesus, the Messiah, writing to exiles scattered to the four winds. Not one is missing, not one forgotten. God the Father has his eye on each of you, and has determined by the work of the Spirit to keep you obedient through the sacrifice of Jesus. May everything good from God be yours!
>
> What a God we have! And how fortunate we are to have him, this Father of our Master Jesus! Because Jesus was raised from the dead, we've been given a brand-new life and have everything to live for, including a future in heaven— and the future starts now! God is keeping careful watch over us and the future. The Day is coming when you'll have it all—life healed and whole.
>
> I know how great this makes you feel, even though you have to put up with every kind of aggravation in the meantime. Pure gold put in the fire comes out of it *proved* pure; genuine faith put through this suffering comes out *proved*

genuine. When Jesus wraps this all up, it's your faith, not your gold, that God will have on display as evidence of his victory.

You never saw him, yet you love him. You still don't see him, yet you trust him—with laughter and singing. Because you kept on believing, you'll get what you're looking forward to: total salvation.[5]

Read this passage again. Now go back and read it five more times! Read it every morning when you get up this week. Read it every night before you go to bed. Read it and think about yourself and the specific people you need to forgive or ask forgiveness from. This is exactly what Jesus wants you to do as he tells the parable in Matthew 18. He wants you to put yourself in the place of the unmerciful servant so that you avoid the terrible error he makes. This parable is a loving warning.

As you ponder your true identity in Christ, do you recognize how wealthy you are? This is the only foundation for the kind of radical forgiveness Jesus calls you to practice. Only by grace can you do this. You can't read and reread 1 Peter 1 and Matthew 18 and still want to rip someone apart. If you are a beneficiary of God's costly grace, you will practice costly grace with others.

Let me close with this real-life illustration. A Turkish officer raided and looted an Armenian home. He killed the aged parents and gave the daughters to the soldiers, keeping the eldest daughter for himself. Some time later she escaped and trained as a nurse. As time passed, she found herself nursing in a ward of Turkish officers. One night, by the light of a lantern, she saw the face of this officer. He was so gravely ill that without exceptional nursing he would die. The days passed, and he recovered. One day, the doctor stood by the bed with her and said to him, "But for her devotion to you, you would be dead." He looked at her and said, "We have met before, haven't we?" "Yes," she said, "we have met before." "Why didn't you kill me?" he asked. She replied, "I am a follower of him who said 'Love your enemies.'"[6]

By God's amazing grace, may we imitate this sister in Christ in our lives and relationships.

---

5   Ibid., 1 Peter 1:1–9.

6   L. Gregory Jones, Embodying Forgiveness: A Theological Analysis (Grand Rapids: Eerdmans, 1995), 265–266.

10

Hope

So justice is far from us,
and righteousness does not reach us.
We look for light, but all is darkness;
for brightness, but we walk in deep shadows.
Like the blind we grope along the wall,
feeling our way like men without eyes.
At midday we stumble as if it were twilight;
among the strong, we are like the dead.
We all growl like bears;
we moan mournfully like doves.
We look for justice, but find none;
for deliverance, but it is far away.

Isaiah 59:9–11

It is always harder to live in the middle of something than it is to live at the beginning or the end. When you are at the beginning of something, you are filled with a sense of hope and potential. You are engaged by a vision of all that can be. People at the start of something tend to be dreamers; they want to get started fulfilling the dream. People at the end tend to be filled with relief, gratitude, and a sense of accomplishment. The hardships along the way don't seem so hard anymore. The sacrifices all seem worth it, and they are glad the work is over.

People in the middle usually discover that more work is involved than they ever expected. It is hard to hold onto the dream, and very often expectation becomes the desire to simply survive. Amidst the hard work, it is difficult to keep your standards high and your hope alive. You are tempted to settle and compromise. In the middle, thankfulness often degrades into complaint, and hope decays into resignation. It is hard to live in the middle of something, but that is exactly where all of our relationships take place. Consider a couple of examples.

As I walked behind him down the hallway to my office, he looked tired. There was no spring left in his step. His slumped shoulders were the testimony of a beaten man. He didn't have to tell me he was discouraged; it was written all over him. It had all blown up in his face again. He had allowed himself to be a bit hopeful, but Thursday night his wife made all her angry threats again. They had made it two weeks without any carnage. He had allowed himself to think that maybe this time they had turned the corner. He was talking to me by himself because she had refused to come with him. But he didn't really want to talk. All he really wanted to do was turn off his pain.

It began when the kids left home. Until then it seemed like they were okay. Sure, they had trouble communicating, but they always seemed to work through it. There probably had been too much conflict between them, but it always seemed to end in forgiveness. There were things about him that irritated her, but he had tried to do better. He had been looking forward to the simpler life they could enjoy now that their primary parenting days were behind them. But it all quickly went sour.

They fought constantly. She enjoyed his company less and less and threatened to leave him every time she was upset. Thursday night she told him she was seriously planning her exit. He couldn't believe it. He had tried to be responsive to her every complaint. They even had gone away together and had a lovely time. After the trip things seemed better. But it had all fallen apart and he was simply exhausted.

Amy was twenty-nine years old and she felt like quitting. She had come from a tough home and had always found it hard to open up to people. She learned early to keep her cards close to the vest and dole out personal information very carefully. She had moved to the big city because of a great job opportunity. Before she accepted the job, she had looked for a good church where she could get involved. Grace Church seemed like the perfect place. It had vibrant biblical preaching, many opportunities for fellowship and ministry, but most of all it was filled with young professionals Amy's age. As she looked around that first Sunday, Amy felt like she saw herself everywhere she looked.

Right after she moved, Amy discovered a Bible study close to her firm that met every Friday during lunch. This Friday study immediately provided a venue for Amy to meet people her age from the church. As always she was cautious, not being too open too soon. But the third time she went, she sat next to Marisa and they struck up a conversation. Before long they were enjoying quite a friendship.

Meanwhile, things at work weren't going so well. Amy loved her job and was receiving lots of kudos for her performance, but she had a big problem. Amy was attracted to her boss. He was good-looking, polite, caring, and funny. She hadn't met a man like him before and, although she tried to restrain her feelings, they persisted. All of this eventually led to a moment of indiscretion with her boss that left Amy crushed. She was convinced that what she had done was wrong, that it had completely robbed her of her boss's respect and possibly compromised her career. Amy's head was spinning, and it got harder and harder to go to work. She knew she needed to talk with someone, so on a park bench in a downtown square, Amy told Marisa everything. Marisa's response was quite helpful, and it felt good not to carry her burden alone.

But the good feelings didn't last. In a brief phone call with another friend, Amy was shocked to learn that Marisa had shared her dilemma with someone else. When she got off the phone, she felt like she couldn't breathe. She couldn't believe that Marisa would be so uncaring and disloyal. She knew she needed to lovingly but clearly confront Marisa, but she had neither the desire nor the energy to do so.

Love's Difficulty

The problem with relationships is that they all take place right smack-dab in the middle of something, and that something is the story of redemption, God's plan to turn everything in our lives into instruments of Christlike change and growth. You and I never get to be married to a fully sanctified spouse. We will never be in a relationship with a completely mature friend. We will never live next to a neighbor utterly free of the need to grow and change. We will never have self-parenting children. We will never be near people who always think, desire, say, or do the right things. And the reason for all of this is that our relationships are lived between the *already* and the *not yet*.

Already Jesus has come to provide salvation for us, but his saving work is *not yet* complete. Already the power of sin has been broken, but the presence of sin has not yet been eradicated. Already we have grown and changed in many ways, but we are not yet all we will be in Christ. Already we have passed through much difficulty, but we have not yet climbed our final hill. Already we have learned many lessons of faith, but we have not yet learned to trust God fully. Already God has established his kingdom in our hearts, but that kingdom has not yet fully come. Already we have seen the defeat of sin in many ways, but its final defeat has not yet taken place.

Our life with others is always life in the middle. We are always building community in the tension between God's "already"and "not yet" grace. And we have no more control over the not yet than we have had over the already. The timetable is in the hands of the sovereign Lord of grace. His timing is always right and he never gets a wrong address. Our job is to learn how to best live in the middle. So we live as broken people who are being repaired, among neighbors in the same condition—always thankful for what has already been done, but ever aware of our need for what we have not yet been given.

Relationships in the Middle

Everyone who lives between the *already* and the *not yet* will experience four things.

Our relationships will never work according to our plan

We've acknowledged before that none of us could write the story of our relationships because they are part of the larger story of redemption. Our relationships don't work according to our plan because they are part of his plan. This means that God will take us where we have not planned to go in order to produce in us what we could not achieve on our own. He will lead us through the hardships so that we will become more and more like him. Many of these hardships will be in relationships, where God reveals our hearts and builds our character. Consequently, our relationships are never what we conceive and never follow the course we plan.

Our relationships will never live up to our expectations

As we look forward to our relationships, we tend to dream of unchallenged unity, unfettered romance, unobstructed communication, mutual cooperation, blanket acceptance and respect, shared decisions, intimate friendship, or an absence of conflict. Our dreams tend to forget that our relationships are being lived out in the middle of the already and the not yet. This side of eternity, none of us get to be with the person of our dreams and none of us are ready to be the person of someone else's dreams! We are all flawed people living in a fallen world, but with a faithful God. And at some point in every relationship, we are required to accept graciously who the other person is, even as we humbly admit who we are.

Our relationships will always grapple with some kind of difficulty

Building relationships is often like threading a needle while driving on a bumpy road! No relationship will be completely successful in avoiding the difficulties that are a normal part of life. Sometimes the difficulty will be the other person. Pride, selfishness, greed, anger, bitterness, and impatience always make a relationship more difficult. Sometimes the difficulty will reflect the reality of a fallen world. Even as believers, we will not escape racism, persecution, injuries, disease, war, mechanical failures, and problems of culture, government, and the economy. Finally, the Bible says that there is a way in which all difficulty is sent by God, in that everything is under his wise control. Along with that, the Bible continually reminds us that God sends the uncomfortable grace of trial not to crush or discourage us, but to mature and refine us. As we are realistic about difficulty, that needs to be our hope.

Our relationships will always need to improve

My wife and I have been married for many years, and we really have a very good relationship. We respect and enjoy each other, we are committed to each other and to the Lord, and we are both very thankful for each other. But after all these years and all the growth we have experienced, our relationship is not yet all it could be. There is still work to be done and changes to be made. For all of our love and commitment, we have not yet escaped our sin, so our relationship still requires hard work and the resources of God's grace. These needs will remain until Christ returns or he takes us home to be with him.

Character for the Middle

Because our relationships are always lived out in the middle of some kind of difficulty, good relationships demand character. Remember, your relationships have not been designed by God as vehicles for human happiness, but as instruments of redemption. It isn't enough to ask for the character you need to survive the difficulties of life and the weaknesses of the other person. We have been called to minister to the people that God, in his wisdom, has placed in our lives. He wants to use us as instruments of grace in their lives. To live this way takes character.

It takes humility to live with a sinner in a world of difficulty. It takes gentleness to be part of what God is doing in someone's life and not get in the way. It takes patience to deal with the sin and weakness of those around you. It takes perseverance to be part of change in a relationship because that change is most often a process and rarely an event. It takes forgiveness to move beyond the times you have been mistreated by another. It takes forbearance to continue to love a person, even when you are being provoked. It is hard to respond in kindness when you are treated unkindly. It takes remarkable love to serve the good of the other person and not be distracted by daily needs. (Notice that these character qualities are mentioned throughout the New Testament: Galatians 5:22–26; Ephesians 4:1–3; Philippians 2:1–11; Colossians 3:12–14.)

These are the qualities that characterize a healthy relationship, but we all must admit that these often are not the things that rule our hearts. Our hearts are more often ruled by anger, fear, hurt, self-righteousness, bitterness, and a desire for some form of vengeance.

The Hardship of Relationships in the Middle

Here is the point. The hardship of relationships is not just that they can be difficult. The hardship includes what God calls us to be and do in the middle of the difficulty. God calls each of us to be humble, patient, kind, persevering, and forgiving. God calls us to speak with grace and to act with love, even when the relationship lacks grace and we have not been treated with love.

Because of this, your relationships will take you beyond the boundaries of your normal strength. They will take you beyond the range of your natural abilities and beyond the borders of your natural and acquired wisdom. Relationships will push you beyond the limits of your ability to love, serve, and forgive. They will push you beyond *you*. At times they will beat at the borders of your faith. At times they will exhaust you. In certain situations, your relationships will leave you disappointed and discouraged. They will require what you do not seem to have, but that is exactly as God intended it. That is precisely why he placed these demanding relationships in the middle of the process of sanctification, where God progressively molds us into the likeness of Jesus. When you give up on yourself, you begin to rely on him. When you are willing to abandon your own little dreams, you begin to get excited about his plan. When your way has blown up in your face again, you are ready to see the wisdom of God's way.

Our relationships are not simply designed to make us interdependent with one another. They are intended to drive us to him in humble personal dependency. At some point, every relationship brings you to the end of yourself, and with God there is no healthier place to be. When I am willing to confess how weak I am, I am most ready to reach out for the grace that can only be found in Christ. He was willing to follow his Father's plan and become weak so that, in our moments of weakness, we could receive his strength. This difficulty-weakness-strength dynamic is why we need so much encouragement in our relationships. We get blindsided by the difficulty, discouraged by our weakness, and end up losing sight of what we have been given in Christ.

Encouragement in the Middle

Encouragement is an essential skill of a biblically healthy community. It is rare when encouragement is not timely. But even when we want to encourage another person, our encouragement can fall short. We tend to make two mistakes. First, we think encouragement is primarily about trying to make the person *feel* better, so we say things like,

"Hang on, you can make it."

"It's not really as bad as you think."

"You're not the only one who has faced this."

"It's going to be okay."

"This too will pass."

These statements may offer temporary comfort, but they never lead to lasting change. At best they produce temporary changes of mood that usually melt away when the person is faced again with difficulty.

The second thing we do is to try to encourage the person by *explaining* to him what the problem is and why it is happening. We think that, if the person understands what is going on, he will be less anxious and more able to do things that are helpful and constructive. There are occasions when this is true, but explanation doesn't always comfort me. Sometimes, the more accurate my understanding of a situation, the more discouraged I get. Once I had a superficial understanding, but I now know how deep the problem really is and I am more overwhelmed than ever. It is important to gain insight and understanding, but encouragement must go deeper than this.

Real encouragement is more about *sightedness* than it is about *explanation*. When I talk about sightedness, I am not talking about physical eyes, but the eyes of the heart. God has given us the capacity to "see" unseen spiritual realities that are as real and vital as any physical thing we can see or touch. Spiritual sightedness is a precious gift and an essential life skill. The reason we get overwhelmed and discouraged in relationships is not because we don't understand what is going on. We are discouraged because we don't see Christ.[1]

In our own strength, we see the husband who barely communicates. We see the friend who has been consistently disloyal. We see the child who rebels against every command. We see the boss who is unrelentingly critical. We see the relative who breaks every promise she makes. We see the wife who is bitter and angry. We see the small group frozen in casual relationships. We see neighbors more

---

1   More will be said about this in Chapter 13.

concerned about boundaries than community. Our relationship problems can loom so large that they obstruct our view of the one thing that can give us the hope and courage to go on. *That one thing is Christ.* Encouragement is not just about making people feel and think better; it's about stimulating spiritual imagination. Encouragement gives struggling people the eyes to see an unseen Christ. He is the only reliable hope when the call of relationship has taken me way beyond my own wisdom, strength, and character.

As we live with each other in the middle of the already and the not yet, we need more than elevated emotion and accurate understanding. We need eyes to see this one amazing reality: we are Christ's and he is ours. We need to see that it is spiritually impossible for us to ever be alone. His amazing resources of grace are constantly at our disposal. In him we find the wisdom, strength, and reason for hope that we have been lacking. Far more than happy feelings and accurate understanding, Christ gives me reason to continue in something that would have long since defeated me.

How do we encourage one another in the middle of relational hardship? By giving each other eyes to see three things.

Christ's presence

Your goal here is to help people develop a "Christ is with me" mentality. This perspective on life is captured in Psalm 46:1–2: "God is our refuge and strength, an *ever-present help* in trouble. Therefore we will not fear, though the earth give way and the mountains fall into the heart of the sea" (authors' emphasis). I love the word picture here. Imagine watching the mountains around you crumble and crash into the ocean without being afraid. It's a picture of personal peace, stability, and security, even when cataclysmic things are happening, because I know that our powerful and glorious God is with me. My hope no longer rests on the shoulders of my own wisdom, strength, and character. When I can see Christ, I realize that I have more than myself to rely on. He is here and able to do what I could never do.

Christ's promises

Christ has made promises that can radically alter the way we perceive and respond to relational difficulties. I can encourage you by helping you remember what is promised. These promises should not be viewed as mystical, pie-in-the-sky unrealities, but as an accurate assessment of my true resources as one of God's children. As I try to help people see how the promises of Christ speak into their situation, they often react negatively. They see God's promises as spiritual trickery to make them feel good about something that is bothering them. But Christ's promises are not the vaporous dreams of spiritual sentimentality. They are the true identity of the believer. The promises of the gospel provide the only accurate perspective on what I really need and the only reliable picture of my true potential for change. Encouragement helps people to accurately measure their potential.

Our potential in Christ

When we struggle, we measure our potential. We assess ourselves to see if we have what it takes to get through the difficulty. The problem is that most of us are poor personal accountants. When we add up the things that define our potential, we leave out the most important asset: Christ. The radical truth about our potential is that, as God's children, our potential *is* Christ! To view ourselves any other way is unbiblical and inaccurate. In Galatians 2:20 Paul says, "I have been crucified with Christ and I no longer live, but Christ lives in me. The life I live in the body, I live by faith in the Son of God, who loved me and gave himself for me." That's an accurate assessment of personal potential!

Since all our relationships exist in the middle of the *already* and the *not yet*, encouragement is an essential skill. How committed are you to helping the people near you see Christ? Are you willing and ready to encourage? What would it look like for you to do this? Remember, you have to see him yourself to show him to others. I remember a time that was tough for my wife and me. The responsibilities of marriage, parenting, and ministry seemed more than we could bear. Finances were tight and our car had just broken down. In our discouragement, we were prickly and irritable with each other. Things turned around when we realized that the burdens we faced were blinding us to God's wildly encouraging truths. As we began to remind each other that we were not alone and to reflect together on his promises to us, something happened. Christ brought us together.

Looking at our situation through the lens of his presence and provision changed our view of things and helped us encourage each other. What he could do in us and for us became more important than whatever we wanted at the moment.

Our relationship didn't suddenly become perfect. It was a tough time and we slipped into blindness again more than once, but we had learned something. We learned to measure our potential as a couple in a brand-new way. That gave us new courage and new hope, and that in turn began to change our relationship.

11

Burdens

A bruised reed he will not break,
and a smoldering wick he will not snuff out.
In faithfulness he will bring forth justice.

Isaiah 42:3

Andrew is the one who taught me that what I believe is not what I say I believe; what I believe is what I do . . . . I am learning to believe better things. I am learning to believe that other people exist, that fashion is not truth; rather, Jesus is the most important figure in history, and the gospel is the most powerful force in the universe. I am learning not to be passionate about empty things, but to cultivate passion for justice, grace, truth, and communicate the idea that Jesus likes people and even loves them.[1]

Words can be powerful or they can be cheap. What makes words powerful is the action that flows from them. Theology also can be powerful or cheap. What makes right thinking about God powerful is the life that emerges daily from that theology. I must confess that this is one of the hardest things about the Christian life for me!

---

1   Donald Miller, *Blue Like Jazz: Nonreligious Thoughts on Christian Spirituality* (Nashville: Thomas Nelson, 2003), 110, 112.

James and John before Jesus's Death and Resurrection

We have talked a lot about thinking the right way about the gospel, and we have been illustrating what right belief should look like in our relationships. Our theology is on display not in our words, but in how we treat others. James and John had to learn this as they jockeyed for position in Christ's kingdom (Mark 10:35–45). When they asked if they could sit at Jesus's left and right hand in heaven, Jesus response turned their expectations upside down.

> When the other ten heard of this conversation, they lost their tempers with James and John. Jesus got them together to settle things down." You've observed how godless rulers throw their weight around," he said," and when people get a little power how quickly it goes to their heads. It's not going to be that way with you. Whoever wants to be great must become a servant. Whoever wants to be first among you must be your slave. That is what the Son of Man has done: He came to serve, not to be served—and then to give away his life in exchange for many who are held hostage."[2]

This was one of those critical teaching moments that Jesus was so good at seizing. Here Jesus communicated something radical about life in his kingdom. Look how fundamentally different it is from life in any earthly kingdom. The pathway to greatness is downward. The pathway to greatness is humility. But more than that, the pathway to greatness is found in serving others.

If our relationships are going to produce Christlike character in us and if Christian community is going to flourish, it is going to take lots of people who relish being demoted in the eyes of the world. Imagine human beings who naturally want position, power, and recognition being transformed into people who gladly throw off self-glory and self-love to be servants in the image of Jesus. This is what will turn average relationships into something glorious. Serving others is a simple way of consolidating all the Bible's "one another" passages under one big idea. When we serve one another, we carry one another's burdens in practical ways. We get our hands dirty as we come alongside people

---

2   Eugene Peterson, *The Message* (Colorado Springs, CO: NavPress, 1993), Mark 10:41–45.

and pay attention to the details of their lives. If our professed commitment to Jesus does not lead us to resemble him in our actions, then we are mocking him and not representing him accurately to the world.

When you think about your relationships, how many of them ultimately revolve around making sure your concerns are heard and your self-defined "needs" are met? Start with those you love the most. I am married and have four children, and most of the time I am committed to thinking about how they can make my life more fulfilling. I know this is true because of how easily I get irritated when I have to give up personal comfort to serve them. This is with people I say I love; I haven't even begun to think about the difficult people. And let's not even bring up our enemies! Do you see this in yourself? This is the first step to becoming a servant. You have to see how much of a servant you aren't before you can start to become one. That is the abiding irony of the Christian life. Up is down, life is death, and power is found and expressed in serving.

The Character and Actions of a Servant

The disciples had to learn this too, which means we are in good company. Here were twelve normal men who spent several years in Jesus's presence, and yet they were so thick-headed that they were vying for power and position. There is a poignant moment in Jesus's ministry when it becomes obvious to the disciples what it means to follow him. John 13:1–17 describes Jesus doing something on the eve of his crucifixion that stuns the disciples and actually offends Peter. What does Jesus do? What does he want his followers to understand as he prepares for his death? In a situation like this, you might expect a leader to rally his followers and give them instructions that will help them change the world. Jesus is doing this, but in his own surprising way. He does it with words and actions.

> Just before the Passover Feast, Jesus knew that the time had come to leave this world to go to the Father. Having loved his dear companions, he continued to love them right to the end. It was suppertime. The Devil by now had Judas, son of Simon the Iscariot, firmly in his grip, all set for the betrayal.

Jesus knew that the Father had put him in complete charge of everything, that he came from God and was on his way back to God. So he got up from the supper table, set aside his robe, and put on an apron. Then he poured water into a basin and began to wash the feet of the disciples, drying them with his apron. When he got to Simon Peter, Peter said, "Master, *you* wash *my* feet?"

Jesus answered,"You don't understand now what I'm doing, but it will be clear enough to you later."

Peter persisted,"You're not going to wash my feet—ever!"

Jesus said, "If I don't wash you, you can't be part of what I'm doing."

"Master!" said Peter."Not only my feet, then. Wash my hands! Wash my head!"

Jesus said, "If you've had a bath in the morning, you only need your feet washed now and you're clean from head to toe. My concern, you understand, is holiness, not hygiene. So now you're clean. But not every one of you."(He knew who was betraying him. That's why he said, "Not every one of you.")

After he had finished washing their feet, he took his robe, put it back on, and went back to his place at the table.

Then he said, "Do you understand what I have done to you? You address me as 'Teacher' and 'Master,' and rightly so. That is what I am. So if I, the Master and Teacher, washed your feet, you must now wash each other's feet. I've laid down a pattern for you. What I've done, you do. I'm only pointing out the obvious. A servant is not ranked above his master; an employee doesn't give orders to the employer. If you understand what I'm telling you, act like it—and live a blessed life."[3]

This is a startling passage. As with all of Scripture, it is designed to disturb the comfortable and comfort the disturbed. When properly understood, both should happen in the same person. What do we learn about what it means to be a leader from this passage? What do we learn about ourselves as we look at the lives of the disciples? What will

---

3   Ibid., John 13:1–17.

motivate us to love in this way? Applying these answers to your life will transform you and bring new vision and vitality to your relationships.

Circumstances Don't Determine Whether You Serve

One of my most common excuses for not being more loving and helpful is my circumstances. When you are weighed down with difficulties, what is the first thing you want to do? You don't want to do *anything*. You want others to do things for you. You want to be served, not serve. Again, I only have to look back as far as yesterday for examples. When my children press in on me the second they arrive from school, I am suddenly reminded of all my responsibilities. *Don't they understand I have a job with many things to think about? Why do they insist that I help them with their homework immediately? Don't they see I have more important things to be concerned about than their assignments?* These are the thoughts that race through my mind. Soon I feel convicted about my impatience and try to rationalize it. *I would be more patient if I didn't have to worry about paying the bills and getting my work done. I would be a kinder, gentler father if they would be less aggressive and more obedient and respectful.* In other words, if my circumstances were easier, I would be a better servant. If I could take care of my cares, I would be more caring. In fact, my children just got home from school as I was writing this, and I was tempted to get irritable—again!

When we encounter Jesus in John 13, his circumstances are horrible. Jesus knew that the hour had come for him to die on the cross for self-centered sinners. He knew that the wrath of a just and holy God would soon fall on him. The just punishment for all his people's sins would crush him in just a few days. Yet what does he do? He serves. He does for his disciples what they should be doing for him. He takes a towel and a basin of water and begins to wash their feet. It would have been very tempting for Jesus to say, "Don't you guys know what is about to happen to me? Get a grip and comfort me!" Yet he says nothing about what is about to happen to him; he just serves, without self-pity. He is utterly selfless at the moment it would be most tempting to be selfish.

That is not normal! Actually, it's downright miraculous. When our circumstances are difficult, it feels like a miraculous act to serve someone else. But that is what Jesus did, and he calls his followers to do the same. We should never minimize the humble service of one person to another; it is a sign of God's grace at work in a person's life.

Someone's Worthiness Does Not Determine Whether You Serve

Jesus not only serves in the midst of his greatest crisis, he serves the very ones who don't deserve to be served. As Jesus's eyes scanned the room, I wonder what he was thinking. He saw Judas, who would soon betray him and hand him over to the Roman authorities. He saw Peter, who would soon deny that he was ever associated with Jesus. The other ten disciples would use the feet he was washing to run for cover when Jesus needed them most. And yet Jesus got down on his knees and served them all.

It is tempting to use my circumstances as an excuse to avoid service. It is equally tempting to size someone up and decide not to serve because you don't think he deserves it or will appreciate it. You don't have to be in ministry very long before you meet self-centered people who think it is your job to respond to their every beck and call. There will be people for whom you pour out your life, who then turn around and say you haven't done enough. Those kinds of people really don't deserve my service. In fact, they drive me crazy!

Maybe you are the kind of person who thinks you can get along with just about anyone. If that is the case, you either haven't lived very long or you have been able to shield yourself from most other humans! But, eventually, someone will enter your life and push you to a place you have never been pushed. Or perhaps you are someone who has ventured into people's lives and been burned—badly. You have vowed never to place yourself in a vulnerable relationship again. You have become cold, careful, and protective. Jesus is calling you to move into people's lives and become vulnerable. He does not say it will be easy, but he does say that this is the only place to find life. You find your life by dying to yourself and caring for others in risky ways.

We can thank God that Jesus moved toward his disciples whether they deserved it or not. Romans 5:8 says, "While we were still sinners, Christ died for us." Who tempts you to give up? Who has maxed out their compassion quota? Jesus is calling you to serve those people. When we model this kind of love, it is compelling evidence that we truly believe what we say. When we serve those who don't deserve it, we are changed and God uses it powerfully in others' lives. Think about the one or two people who have most significantly impacted your life for good. Weren't humility and servanthood a large part of their influence? Those two qualities catch us by surprise and make us want to be that way for others. They are a powerful influence.

I am forty-four. I have had twenty-plus years to reflect on how my parents served me. But I needed to be married myself, with children of my own, before I could catch a glimpse of all they did for me as I was growing up. As I see it more clearly, it compels and motivates me to quietly serve my own children. Thus my parents' service is now spilling over into the lives of my children. Jesus served because it was the right thing to do, but he also knew it was the only way his disciples would be freed from the hollow pursuit of personal glory and the enslaving nature of self-love. What an impact this had on the disciples and the world!

Your Position Doesn't Determine Whether You Serve

Now we get to the most amazing part of this story. Remember, Jesus knew who he was. In John 13:1, Jesus knows he is about to return to the Father. In verse 3, he knows he is the King of the universe. In other words, Jesus knew he was God. He owed no one anything. He was sufficient in himself and needed no one. And yet he chose to humble himself and wash the disciples' feet. This amazing act would be overshadowed only by the humiliation he would voluntarily endure on the cross.

Our culture feeds us the lie that the main goal in life is to climb the ladder of power and influence. It tells us to look to Donald Trump or others like him if we want to be great. We think that purpose, fulfillment, and meaning are found in ascending. But Jesus says that all those things are found in descending. Jesus and his kingdom are on a collision course with the values of this fallen world, and he is calling us to align with him.

If Jesus is right and you claim to acknowledge him as your Savior and King, how are you doing in terms of your greatness? When did you serve this past week when the world would say you should have been served? I can't think of any relationship where this notion is more frequently put to the test than with my children. The Bible clearly says that parents have authority over their children. Children are not to run the household; parents are. It would seem to follow that children are to serve their parents. Yet, at the same time, the Bible redeems authority from sinful patterns by humbling parents and calling them to use their authority for the benefit of the child. I have daily opportunities to gauge the sincerity of my stated beliefs in Jesus. Sadly, those beliefs are often out of sync with my actions. But there are times, because of God's grace, when my beliefs and deeds are joined together harmoniously, and I thank God for them! Where in your life do you have the privilege to serve people who are "under" you?

Power for Servants

The story of Jesus washing the disciples' feet should overwhelm you. If you were comfortable when you started reading this chapter, you burdens should be very disturbed now! Are you seeing how pervasive your self-centeredness is in your relationships? Every time I read John 13, I see my heap of daily failures. I see how "me-centered" I am, even when I think I am serving. Nevertheless, despite our self-centeredness, in verses 14 and 15 Jesus still calls us to this kind of humble service. This can be overwhelming, but it can also help us see that we are not sufficient in ourselves to behave this way. We see our need for God's power and grace to change.

Although the disciples didn't understand what Jesus was doing at the time, after his resurrection and the coming of the Holy Spirit, everything made sense to them. This was not because they had new cognitive insights that changed them into servants. They were radically changed because they experienced the inner spiritual transformation brought about by Jesus's work on their behalf. What the disciples came to "understand" experientially transformed them into totally different men. We need the same understanding if we are going to serve people for the long haul.

Foot Washing and the Cross

As Jesus came to wash Peter's feet, Peter could not bear to see Jesus in this place of abject submission. He doesn't allow him to proceed. Jesus explains what he is doing and what it means. In verse 7, Jesus says, "You do not realize now what I am doing, but later you will understand." He then says, as Peter protests, "Unless I wash you, you have no part with me." What do these cryptic words mean? Jesus is saying that what he is doing symbolizes something even greater. His humble service of washing their feet points to what he will do for them on the cross in just a few days. But instead of water, his blood will be poured out as he gives his life for them. The sacrifice of his blood will be the cleansing agent to wash away their sins and make them living temples in which the Holy Spirit dwells. Jesus tells Peter that if he will not humble himself and receive what he is about to do for him on the cross, Peter will have no part with him. Jesus knows that, unless these proud men humble themselves to receive grace, they will never be able to give grace in the way Jesus has served them. Proud sinners who can't receive grace as a gift from God will not be likely to offer it. You can't serve other sinners if you don't receive Jesus's service for you. There is no way you will be up for the task.

The Need for Daily Grace

Jesus says another striking thing in verse 10: "A person who has had a bath needs only to wash his feet; his whole body is clean. And you are clean, though not every one of you." What does Jesus mean? He is speaking about their relationship with God. They have been bathed, meaning they are in a relationship with God by virtue of their simple faith in Jesus, their Savior. In other words, they are justified. But Jesus says that a bath, as important as it is, must be accompanied by daily cleansing. They need the daily grace of sanctification. You and I need the cleansing work of Jesus's life, death, and resurrection applied to our lives daily. You can't live on past grace. You need present grace.

The second you move out into the world, you will face troubles and persecution. You may have to get involved in nasty church disputes between believers, or something equally painful. There will be times when you will wonder whether it is worth following Jesus. At these precise moments, you will need the work of the Spirit in your life to remind you of your own sin and the grace available to you. Repentance and faith must be your daily lifestyle. Why? Because it lays you low and lifts you up at the same time.

When was the last time you were called to serve someone? What moved you in that person's direction? Was it remembering how great you are and how much this person needed to be touched by your greatness? If that is what motivated you, your service was paltry at best. When was the last time you served someone well even though you knew no one would ever see you doing it? What drove you to do it? There had to be, at some level, an awareness of the grace Christ offered you despite your own depravity. As the Holy Spirit worked these truths deep into your heart, you developed a desire to carry someone else's burden. You did it regardless of what you might gain. Only daily grace can have this effect.

As you have reflected on this story, you must see how much you need daily grace. Consider the countless times you have failed others in moments of self-protection and self-glory. If there were no place to run for cleansing and healing, there would be no reason to carry on. But the service Jesus rendered for us in his life, death, and resurrection is not just for forgiveness of sins or a future in heaven; it is also for the daily power to change in the present. We are not just promised life after death, but life before death! You can remember this as you face the realities of life in a broken world.

Promises of Blessing

In John 13:17, Jesus says, "Now that you know these things, you will be blessed if you do them." Blessing comes when knowing and doing intersect, and the Christian life is the most blessed life that can ever be lived. In the movie *Chariots of Fire*, the protagonist Eric Liddell says, "When I run, I feel God's pleasure." Jesus says that when we serve another person, we experience God's pleasure. When Eric Liddell ran, he was living out what God had gifted him to be, a runner. When you and I serve, we are living out what God has made us to be, servants. It is when we are serving that we are most like the Trinity. Father, Son, and Spirit redeemed a fallen world through service and sacrifice. There is nothing more God-like than serving others.

John Revisited

Little is known about John's brother James—tradition has it that he died a martyr's death. But we know that John was a changed person after Jesus's resurrection. This can be seen in his later writings. He is the author of the passage we have been considering, but he also wrote other New Testament letters that focus on the deeds that should accompany our words of faith. The specific deeds he discusses are deeds toward people. Read how he puts it in 1 John 3:16–18:

> This is how we've come to understand and experience love: Christ sacrificed his life for us. This is why we ought to live sacrificially for our fellow believers, and not just be out for ourselves. If you see some brother or sister in need and have the means to do something about it but turn a cold shoulder and do nothing, what happens to God's love? It disappears. And you made it disappear.
>
> My dear children, let's not just talk about love; let's practice real love.[4]

No doubt about it, John is talking and acting very differently than he did in Mark 10. What changed him so radically? The practical, sacrificial service of Jesus on the cross and all of the blessings that flow from his work. If there is hope for a man like John, there is hope for you and me. What Jesus did for John as his living Lord and Savior is nothing short of miraculous. He was forgiven, adopted, and filled with the Spirit. God promised to protect and care for him in this life and to one day free him from sin altogether so he could love Father, Son, and Spirit forever. This is what changed John; this is what can change you and me. This is the good news of the gospel. Jesus has come for sinners to begin a process of total transformation that will end in us exhibiting the very character of Jesus.

Serving Others

The following "one another" passages can help you apply what you have read in this chapter. Take a moment to reflect on a few specific relationships in your life. You may want to consider three: a loved one, a difficult person you usually avoid, and an enemy. With these people in mind, consider these passages and the practical commands they give. Evaluate how you are doing. Reflect on Christ's grace and service to you. Think of ways you can serve these people in the coming months.

---

4   Ibid., 1 John 3:16–18.

Be devoted to one another

Romans 12:10 says, "Be devoted to one another in brotherly love." This means that we treat other people like they are part of our family, with the kind of mutual love that exists between parents, children, and siblings. Sure, there are family squabbles, but when the heat is on, we rally around our family. Whom do you need to rally around as if they were "blood"? Come to think of it, if they are Christians, the bond between you and them is more than biological. You are united spiritually through your elder brother Jesus. How should this shape your relationships?

Honor one another

Romans 12:10 says, "Honor one another above yourselves." Honoring someone means that you treat her seriously. You treat her as someone of value. Paul suggests doing this by taking a back seat. Jesus came and humbled himself so that we might be lifted up. He did this for you. Whom do you need to treat with honor?

Accept one another

Romans 15:7 says, "Accept one another, then, just as Christ accepted you, in order to bring praise to God." We all differ with one another on a host of issues that are not central to being a Christian. Often these differences become the things we think are most important, and this could easily lead us to distance ourselves from one another. In James 2, the rich were guilty of favoritism. They distanced themselves from those who lacked the same social and economic standing. Whenever we fail to accept others, we lose opportunities to serve. Whom do you tend to exclude? What nonessential, secondary convictions do you allow to get between you and another Christian? In what ways do you need to accept others? Who needs your acceptance right now?

Bear one another's burdens

Galatians 6:2 says, "Carry each other's burdens, and in this way you will fulfill the law of Christ." This command is very practical. In the context of another Christian's struggle, we are called to struggle alongside him. Some of the weight of his burden will fall on you.

It may cut into your lifestyle and require sacrifice. This may mean meeting with someone for a period of time. It may require a financial sacrifice. It may mean both. Where do you need to shoulder someone else's burden? How will that change the way you use your time and money, talents, possessions, and reputation? What other resources do you have that can be used to ease the burden?

Bear with one another

Ephesians 4:2 teaches, "Be completely humble and gentle; be patient, bearing with one another in love." We have already talked about forgiving others when we have been sinned against. Bearing with others is equally important. What does it mean to bear with one another? It means that you are patient with others when you would be tempted to get irritated. What weaknesses and idiosyncrasies do you find hard to tolerate in others? These aren't necessarily sins, just things that get on your nerves. Whom do you find hard to love? What kinds of people do you unconsciously avoid because they simply bug you? Surely you can think of someone! Serving him means a willingness to be tolerant, even when he does things you find bothersome. Remember, you have weaknesses and things that bother others too. Look at how tolerant Jesus was with his disciples. We can be thankful that he is that way with us too.

Serving Others Is Practical

Serving others is the way we put feet on our faith. What we believe is not just what we say; it is inextricably bound to what we do. How are you doing? Is your faith in Jesus expressing itself in your relationships? I earn a living speaking and writing about the Bible. That scares me, because it can appear to others that I am really mature spiritually. I might even start to believe it myself! But am I really mature and growing in grace? Do my actions correspond to all my talk?

What about you? Are you known for knowing a lot about the Bible and doctrine, but not for quiet service to others? If you are a parent, spouse, child, neighbor, or sibling, what will it look like for you to be a servant this week? Humble service is a mark of the Spirit's work in you. May it be increasingly evident in all of us as we grow in grace!

12

Mercy

"Their feet are swift to shed blood;
ruin and misery mark their ways,
and the way of peace they do not know."

Romans 3:15–17

My brothers, as believers in our glorious Lord Jesus Christ, don't show favoritism. Suppose a man comes into your meeting wearing a gold ring and fine clothes, and a poor man in shabby clothes also comes in. If you show special attention to the man wearing fine clothes and say, "Here's a good seat for you," but say to the poor man, "You stand there" or "Sit on the floor by my feet," have you not discriminated among yourselves and become judges with evil thoughts?

Listen, my dear brothers: Has not God chosen those who are poor in the eyes of the world to be rich in faith and to inherit the kingdom he promised those who love him? But you have insulted the poor. Is it not the rich who are exploiting you? Are they not the ones who are dragging you into court? Are they not the ones who are slandering the noble name of him to whom you belong?

If you really keep the royal law found in Scripture, "Love your neighbor as yourself," you are doing right. But if you show favoritism, you sin and are convicted by the law as lawbreakers. For whoever keeps the whole law and yet stumbles at just one point is guilty of breaking all of it. For he who said, "Do not commit adultery," also said, "Do not murder." If you do not commit adultery but do commit murder, you have become a lawbreaker.

Speak and act as those who are going to be judged by the law that gives freedom, because judgment without mercy will be shown to anyone who has not been merciful. Mercy triumphs over judgment! (James 2:1–13)

We were convinced it was what God had called us to do. We were going to live with an open home commitment to hospitality and view our home as a God-given ministry resource. Most of our ministry guests had been short-term. After a night or so, they would leave and our home would return to comfortable normality. But this time it was different. It had been weeks and there was no end in sight. The problem was that she simply drove me crazy, and despite all my attempts to deal with it, I found her very hard to take.

We had gotten the call late on Sunday evening. She was seventeen. She had been thrown out of her house and was getting ready to bed down in a local park. Besides being embarrassed and unsure of what she was getting into that night, she was hurt, angry, and afraid. In a few days it became clear that she could not go back home and she had no other options. So, out of a combined belief in the sovereignty of God and a call to mercy, we committed ourselves for the long haul. We were excited because God was giving us an opportunity to do what we had committed ourselves to do. We were motivated by the ways God could use this to transform this young woman's life. We really loved the fact that God saw our home as a ministry tool, and we were ready to learn, on the job, exactly what that meant.

The problem was that she tried my patience like few people have. We introduced her to the people at our church and then in our small group. Everyone immediately took her in and seemed enthused with what we were doing. We got to know her story, communicated with her family, and began to help her think about how she had gotten to this point and how she needed to prepare for the future. The longer she stayed, the more candid our conversations became. We could see change beginning to take place in her perspectives on herself and on life in general, and we began to see her spiritual interest grow. But despite all these positive things going on, she could still really get on my nerves.

She was immature, self-centered, rebellious, rude, illogical, messy, and nosy. I had never lived with anyone with all of those qualities in one package! It seemed that if she improved in one area, she would irritate me in another. There wasn't much she did right, and almost nothing she said came out sounding logical and mature. She obviously needed some authority in her life, but she rebelled against even the insignificant rules of our home. She argued with anyone who would presume to give her guidance. She left a trail of chaos behind her wherever she went and seemed to be allergic to domestic chores of any kind. She had made a series of horrible decisions that literally left her on the street, but she was quick to defend each one. She had a very small universe, but she was at its center. She lived as if it really was "all about her." On top of it all, she seemed dedicated to intrude upon whatever shreds of privacy we had left. She had a gift for bringing out the worst in me, although she never seemed to know it and would probably say we had a good relationship.

Mercy's Struggle

There is a corollary to Murphy's Law that says, "Everything you decide to do costs more than you first estimated." So it is with ministry. If you have a commitment to do more than just survive the people around you, an agenda higher than your own happiness, and a desire to be an instrument in God's hands, you will soon learn that the cost of ministry always exceeds your preliminary calculations. The same is true for mercy.

A relationship without mercy is a relationship lived outside biblical borders. God clearly calls us to respond to one another out of a heart of mercy. He commands us to extend the same mercy to others that we have received from him. The problem is that mercy is hard. That was my problem with our houseguest. I wanted to live with an open home and touch people's lives. I just didn't think it would be so hard!

Someone once said that mercy is a commodity that everyone desires but no one wants to give. Yet God had brought me to a point where I didn't want to just receive mercy; I saw the value of giving it as well. I wanted our home to be a place where mercy could be found.

I felt sympathy for those less fortunate. I wanted to use what God had given us to relieve their distress, and I wanted our mercy to introduce them to God's mercy. But mercy is more costly than we imagine, and when that bill comes in, we tend to be less enamored by its beauty. That was my situation.

As you extend mercy and encounter its heavy cost, you will see how thin your commitment to mercy is and how unmerciful your responses can be. It's very humbling, but a commitment to mercy will reveal your own need for mercy. Unfortunately, that is something we often prefer not to see. We want to think of ourselves as fundamentally different from the people who need mercy when, in fact, we are the same. We too are flawed people; we too need mercy every day of our lives. But it is more comfortable to think of ourselves as righteous and strong while others are needy and weak. So, when it comes to mercy, we are double-minded. We'd rather give mercy than need it, but even then, we wish the giving wasn't so costly—and revealing.

From God's point of view, one of the most beneficial aspects of mercy is that it levels the playing field. Mercy forces us all to face the fact that we need it. None of us has the spiritual upper hand. In our struggle with sin, we all need compassion, sympathy, forgiveness, and rescue. All of us are poor in some way, lacking things we desperately need. Each of us lives with weakness and the results of our own poor choices. But even when we seem to have it right, even when we are committed to live in mercy, we struggle to love the very people we have looked on with sympathy. And even while we are basking in God's forgiveness, we find it incredibly difficult to bear with the sin and weakness of others. That's why, in the mirror of mercy, all of us tend to look the same.

What Is Mercy Anyway?

I once asked a retreat crowd to define faith for me. The first person said, "Well, it means to believe." I said, "What does it mean to believe?" A second person chimed in, "To believe means to trust." So I said, "What does it mean to trust?" And someone said, "It means to have faith!" We had come full-circle in three steps and not come any closer to defining faith. So it is with mercy. It is one of those biblical terms that every believer has heard, many use, but few can properly define. Therefore, I want to give you two definitions of mercy: (1)

Mercy is the kind, sympathetic, and forgiving treatment of others that works to relieve their distress and cancel their debt. Or (2) mercy is compassion combined with forbearance and action.

These two definitions tell us a lot about what mercy is, why it is needed, and how it expresses itself. Mercy is much more than the pang of sympathy you momentarily feel when you walk by the homeless panhandler on the street. It quickly crosses your mind that it must be tough to have nowhere to live. You wonder for a second how he does it; and, as you pass by, you are relieved that you are not in his situation. A moment later, you have forgotten him, and you and your friends are talking about the great restaurant you are going to that night. You may have felt momentary sympathy, but your actions lack mercy. What makes mercy merciful is a heartfelt compassion that results in some kind of action toward the other person. Mercy is not just something you feel; mercy is something you do. It is a lifestyle, a stance toward others that shapes everything we say and do.

Mercy has eyes. It pays attention to your distress and notices your weaknesses and failures. But mercy looks at these things with eyes of compassion. It doesn't criticize you for the tough situation you are in or condemn you for your sin. Mercy wants to relieve your suffering and forgive your debt. It looks for ways to help you out of your struggle and remove your guilt and shame. Real mercy is restless. It is not content with the status quo. It doesn't rest until things are better for you. It works hard, costs a lot, and is ready to hang on until the job is done.

Mercy is driven by three character qualities:

- **Compassion.** Compassion is a deep awareness of another's suffering that leads to a desire to help. Compassion sees beyond one's own difficulties to care about the difficulties of others.
- **Forgiveness.** Forgiveness pardons a person for an offense without treating him like a criminal or harboring resentment against him.
- **Forbearance.** Forbearance is patience under provocation. It is willing to stand alongside someone in trouble, even though it makes life more difficult.

Mercy looks at the trouble of others and cares, acts, forgives, and perseveres.

What Makes Mercy So Essential?

Like many other qualities of a good relationship, mercy is essential because our relationships take place in the middle of the great redemptive story. We live in a fallen world and face difficulty and distress while we simultaneously struggle with the sin that remains in us. Mercy is needed because neither the world we live in nor the people who inhabit it are perfect.

None of us could live in a world where there was only justice. Because of our sin, none of us is ready to have pure justice exercised in our direction. Without mercy, we would all be doomed! So until God's kingdom comes, he withholds his final justice. He gives us one more day to confess and turn from wrong. He is amazingly patient, infinitely kind, and incredibly forgiving. His compassion causes his justice to wait and his mercy to act. And since God has decided to respond to his world with mercy, this gives us more of a call to be merciful ourselves. Yet we tend to get mercy and justice all mixed up. We want mercy for ourselves because we want our lives to be comfortable, and we want justice for the other guy because we want our lives to be comfortable. As self-absorbed sinners, we simply don't want to deal with distressed and flawed people. But it is impossible to have relationships without being troubled by the trouble of others.

The Bible's teaching on mercy is clear. Until God's kingdom comes and everything broken is restored, there will continue to be suffering. As long as God chooses to give sinners one more opportunity to repent, the distress of living in a fallen world will continue. That is why mercy is an essential ingredient of any godly relationship. Mercy is what we have received and what we are called to give. Mercy is my commitment to live alongside you in this broken world, even though I will suffer with you, for you, and because of you. I will do everything I can to relieve your distress.

Your Relationships and Mercy's Agenda

A commitment to mercy will change your relationships, just as it will change you. Let's consider how a practical commitment to mercy sets a new agenda for your relational life.

Mercy means you expect suffering in your relationships and are willing to endure it

It includes a willingness to have your life distressed by the weakness and distress of others. Mercy means I will stand near my teenager, even when his wardrobe embarrasses me and his spiritual lostness troubles my heart. Mercy means I will persevere with a spouse with more weaknesses than I realized when we got married. Mercy means I will love someone whose manners offend me. It includes a willingness to get involved in someone's life, even when it means personal inconvenience and sacrifice. *Do your relationships demonstrate a willingness to suffer for another's sake?*

Mercy means you are willing to live with the poor

James 2 makes this very clear. Often the great struggle with mercy is its call to relate to people we consider beneath us. Often, when we discover the "poverty" of another, we get disenchanted with the relationship and plan our exit. Keep in mind that poverty is not always economic. A person can be difficult to live with because he is spiritually or socially poor. The point is, when you are in a relationship with someone, his "poverty" will become your firsthand experience. This is when a commitment to mercy will expose your faulty thinking. You and I tend to see ourselves as "rich" and the other person as "poor." The spiritual reality is that we are both poor: neither of us would make it in a world devoid of mercy! *Do your attitudes and responses change when you discover that a person is "poor" in some way?*

Mercy means you resist the temptation to favoritism

James 2 is a frontal assault on one of Christianity's most frequent idolatries, favoritism. We thank God for his acceptance even though we are messed up, difficult people, yet we tend to surround ourselves with people who are easy to like and who like us in return. We get frustrated when the "easy" people prove not to be so easy after all. It is tempting for a parent to favor a more compliant child, or a friend to favor a more "together" friend, or a small group to be more excited when a wealthy couple joins than when an addicted man begins attending. If we are only committed to be hospitable to people we find comfortable, our lives still lack mercy. *Are there relationships in which you have indulged in favoritism?*

Mercy means you are committed to persevere in hardship

Mercy sees hardship and does not run away. It jumps in and gets involved. Mercy does its best work when suffering is apparent or forgiveness is needed. It doesn't look for a way out just because things have suddenly gotten hard. Mercy that does not persevere isn't mercy. There are no ideal relationships out there. We all are called to persevere through painful things in order to be part of what God is doing. *In your relationships, where are you struggling with God's call to persevere?*

Mercy rejects a "personal happiness" agenda

If I want my relationships to meet my needs or if I am living for comfort and ease, I will not extend mercy when the going gets tough. Mercy means living for an agenda higher than my present happiness. Mercy is willing to involve itself in things that are not happy or comfortable. It finds more joy in doing God's will than in a comfortable, predictable life. Mercy is willing to forsake comfort to bring God's comfort to someone else. It finds more fulfillment in the progress of the kingdom of God than it does in the development of the kingdom of man. It is always more motivated by what God is seeking to do in a relationship than by what we think we can get out of it. *Where is God calling you to leave what is comfortable so that you can share what he has given you with another?*

Mercy means you live with a commitment to forgive

Whenever you are involved with people who need mercy, you will inevitably be sinned against. When I commit myself to love you, your sin and struggles will become my firsthand experience. One reason we play favorites is that we don't want to relate to people who will need our forgiveness. But mercy means that I am so grateful for the daily forgiveness I receive that I cannot help offering you the same. My actions and attitudes are governed by a humble recognition that everything I am offering, I also desperately need. *Are there people in your life you are struggling to forgive?*

Mercy means you overlook minor offenses

It is tempting to focus on the irritating things another person does while excusing my own minor offenses. But mercy isn't hypervigilant, easily irritated, or quickly offended. Mercy is so engaged by the beauty of the big things God is doing that it doesn't have time to focus on things that are of no consequence. *Where have you allowed yourself to be distracted and irritated by the minor offenses of others?*

Mercy does not compromise what is morally right and true

Extending mercy doesn't mean I turn my back on God's law. Reaching out to you in mercy doesn't require me to forsake what is morally right and true. Mercy means that, if you are caught in sin, I will not ignore your plight, get mad, or abandon you, but I will still point you to God and the promises and principles of his Word. My willingness to persevere and forgive reflects my desire to give God room to do the good things only he can do in your life. Mercy understands that grace is a better pathway to change than condemnation, but it never compromises what is morally right and true. *Are there places where you have confused compromise with mercy?*

A commitment to mercy will reveal the treasures of your heart

Why do we struggle with offering mercy? We struggle because there are things we desire more than God and his glory. Our struggle reveals that our hearts are ruled more by comfort, appreciation, respect, love, success, control, achievement, possessions, position, power, and acceptance than we have been willing to admit. Here is the painful spiritual reality: our struggle with mercy is not just a second great command struggle; it is a first great command struggle as well. We struggle to respond rightly to one another because we don't have God in the right place. Mercy in our relationships has been compromised by the subtle pursuit of various god replacements. *Do your desires get in the way of offering mercy to others?*

Giving mercy always demands mercy

When you extend mercy, you will begin to see how selfish, impatient, unforgiving, and inconsistent you can be. Mercy will show you how much your own heart still needs the continuing work of the Redeemer. It will drive you to the end of yourself and to the grace of your merciful Savior. And that is a very good thing!

The Rest of the Story

The seventeen-year-old girl who lived in our home is now a grown woman with children of her own. She is still a part of our lives. While she was with us, God radically changed her heart and her life's direction. But I cannot look back on those tough days and think only of her. Usually, my mind goes to me and my Lord. In calling me to mercy, God was actually extending mercy to me. He wasn't sacrificing his work in me to accomplish something worthwhile in her. When God chose me to be his instrument of mercy, it was not just a call to duty; it was a gift of grace. Even though I wasn't very willing and often blew it along the way, I am so glad for God's determined grace! He enabled us to stay the course, even though at times I resisted. He was merciful—to her and to me.

13

Time and Money

Man is a mere phantom as he goes to and fro:
He bustles about, but only in vain;
he heaps up wealth, not knowing who will get it.
Psalm 39:6

If you want to discover what you treasure, look at your schedule and checkbook. How you relate to time and money says a lot about your relationship with God. It also speaks volumes about how you view other people. Ephesians 4:28 and 5:16 say important things about money and time. And interestingly, Paul slips these comments in amid teaching on relationships. He does this because the way we deal with our money and time has a significant impact on our relationships.

Before we look closely at these verses, we must step back to get the big picture. You can't think about anything correctly unless you see it as a whole. And since God is the whole, we need to start with him.

God's glory is the most important thing to him. God is jealous for his reputation in a way that is completely right and exclusive to him. He wants his fame to spread throughout the entire universe. He intends to establish his perfect, glorious kingdom over everything he has made, and he sent Jesus to bring this kingdom to earth. But if God is committed to bringing his kingly rule to earth, and he is truly God, why can't he just do it immediately? He can, but if he did, all of sinful humanity would be wiped out. Instead, he emptied heaven of its greatest treasure to redeem us so that we could have a place in his kingdom when he comes to establish it once and for all. Father, Son, and Spirit graciously included human beings in the kingdom by dealing with the sin that separated us from God. God spent his most precious treasure, his only Son Jesus, to redeem us from ourselves and the tyranny of sin. This demonstrates God's commitment to his own glory, his intention to display his glory through his kingdom, and his plan to make us a vital part of that display. How important is God's fame or glory to you? The answer to this question can be seen, partly in the way you invest your time and money. It isn't complicated, but it isn't easy either.

Money and People

As we mentioned, Ephesians 4:28 is part of a broader discussion about relationships.

> Therefore each of you must put off falsehood and speak truthfully to his neighbor, for we are all members of one body. "In your anger do not sin": Do not let the sun go down while you are still angry, and do not give the devil a foothold. *He who has been stealing must steal no longer, but must work, doing something useful with his own hands, that he may have something to share with those in need.*
>
> Do not let any unwholesome talk come out of your mouths, but only what is helpful for building others up according to their needs, that it may benefit those who listen. And do not grieve the Holy Spirit of God, with whom you were sealed for the day of redemption. Get rid of all bitterness, rage and anger, brawling and slander, along with every form of malice. Be kind and compassionate to one another, forgiving each other, just as in Christ God forgave you. (Ephesians 4:25–32, authors' emphasis)

Why would Paul insert a comment about giving into a discussion of relationships? The passage talks about being "members of one body" in verse 25, and follows with practical applications that have our relationships in full view.

Paul is posing the question, "How can you tell whether you love people?" Another way to think about verse 28 is to ask, "When has a thief stopped being a thief?" Is it when he stops stealing? Is it when he stops stealing and gets a job? A thief is no longer a thief when he stops stealing, gets a job, and begins giving to others. This is just another way of unpacking the eighth commandment, "You shall not steal." There is a negative side and a positive side to the command: stop doing something and start doing something else. It is the "put off" and "put on" Paul talks so much about in his epistles. Paul is saying that we haven't really started loving others with our money until we start giving it away to help them! It is good to stop stealing. It is good to get a job. But you haven't stopped being a thief until a part of your money goes to help people besides yourself.

Look at your relationship to money. From what you see, what can you conclude about your relationship with God? Does he function as the One who provides all your needs? Is he the One you trust for security? What do your investments say about how you think about yourself and others? Good financial planning can be a wise way to care for others in the future. But what are you investing in right now, in addition to your portfolio? Is there any indication that you are investing your money in the things God says are most important? Or are you just building bigger and better barns that only serve your purposes?

Increasing Wealth, Declining Giving

Put these issues in the social and historical context in which many of us live. The average American today makes four times what the average American made in 1921 after adjusting for taxes and inflation. Real incomes have doubled since the late 1950s. Today's average, middleclass citizen lives like the rich banker of our grandparents' generation. We have more clothes and bigger homes, and we dine out regularly. Granted, most Americans are very generous compared to citizens of other nations. But by biblical standards, we are not generous at all. Over the past twenty years, seventy percent of Americans only gave one or two percent of their income to charitable causes. Thirty percent do not give at all! People who profess to be Christians are not doing much better, giving away only three to four percent of their annual income on average. By percentages, Americans tend to be stingy even though the total amount can make us appear generous.

Signs of Generosity

How can you tell if you are a generous person? The Bible does not leave us guessing when it comes to this very basic mark of spiritual maturity. Both the Old and New Testaments say that you begin to become a generous person when you invest at least ten percent of your income in the things of God. Given God's heart for the lost and suffering of this world, this will inevitably lead you to give to the needs of others as well. This may take many forms, but giving to your local church often allows you to participate in many diverse ministries through the people, programs, and causes it supports.

The Old Testament established the ten percent tithe as the giving threshold for God's people. In the New Testament, Jesus does not rescind the call to tithe. Instead, he calls us to a radical lifestyle of caring for others with our money. In Luke 11:42 Jesus rebukes the Pharisees when he says, "Woe to you Pharisees, because you give God a tenth of your mint, rue and all other kinds of garden herbs, but you neglect justice and the love of God. You should have practiced the latter without leaving the former undone." Notice that Jesus says that we are to give at least a tenth, *as well as* practice justice for those who are helpless! Because of the radical grace we receive from Christ, we are to be radically generous to others. Here are a few ways to examine your own life when it comes to giving. Second Corinthians 8:1–15 is a wonderful picture of gospel generosity.

> Now, friends, I want to report on the surprising and generous ways in which God is working in the churches in Macedonia province. Fierce troubles came down on the people of those churches, pushing them to the very limit. The trial exposed their true colors: They were incredibly happy, though desperately poor. The pressure triggered something totally unexpected: an outpouring of pure and generous gifts. I was there and saw it for myself. They gave offerings of whatever they could—far more than they could afford!—pleading for the privilege of helping out in the relief of poor Christians.

This was totally spontaneous, entirely their own idea, and caught us completely off guard. What explains it was that they had first given themselves unreservedly to God and to us. The other giving simply flowed out of the purposes of God working in their lives. That's what prompted us to ask Titus to bring the relief offering to your attention, so that what was so well begun could be finished up. You do so well in so many things—you trust God, you're articulate, you're insightful, you're passionate, you love us—now, do your best in this, too.

I'm not trying to order you around against your will. But by bringing in the Macedonians' enthusiasm as a stimulus to your love, I am hoping to bring the best out of you. You are familiar with the generosity of our Master, Jesus Christ. Rich as he was, he gave it all away for us—in one stroke he became poor and we became rich.

So here's what I think: The best thing you can do right now is to finish what you started last year and not let those good intentions grow stale. Your heart's been in the right place all along. You've got what it takes to finish it up, so go to it. Once the commitment is clear, you do what you can, not what you can't. The heart regulates the hands. This isn't so others can take it easy while you sweat it out. No, you're shoulder to shoulder with them all the way, your surplus matching their deficit, their surplus matching your deficit. In the end you come out even. As it is written,

"Nothing left over to the one with the most, Nothing lacking to the one with the least."[1]

Paul makes two comparisons that provide clear examples of how to view our giving.

Comparison One: The Giving of the Macedonians

This passage is an example of true kingdom generosity. Look at the Macedonians and compare their relationship with money to your own.

---

1   Eugene Peterson, *The Message* (Colorado Springs, CO: NavPress, 1993), 2 Corinthians 8:1–15.

Their giving encouraged unity

The Macedonians were Gentiles, and they owed their new spiritual life to Jewish Christians. Their giving reflected this. In Romans 15:25–27 Paul says,

> First, though, I'm going to Jerusalem to deliver a relief offering to the Christians there. The Greeks—all the way from the Macedonians in the north to the Achaians in the south—decided they wanted to take up a collection for the poor among the believers in Jerusalem. They were happy to do this, but it was also their duty. Seeing that they got in on all the spiritual gifts that flowed out of the Jerusalem community so generously, it is only right that they do what they can to relieve their poverty.[2]

Here you have a tangible expression of unity between Jewish and Gentile Christians. This is remarkable, given the deep rift that existed between Jew and Gentile even in the early days of the first-century church. Our experience of reconciling grace is expressed every time we pool our resources for the kingdom of God.

Their giving was a supernatural work of the Spirit

Returning to 2 Corinthians 8, in verse 1 Paul says that their giving was a sign of God's work in them. This kind of giving does not happen naturally. Their unified worship of the living God produced giving that was surprising and even shocking.

Their giving was surprising

The Macedonians gave contrary to the way the world gives. They gave not out of abundance, but despite their own need. In the midst of their own poverty and persecution, they exhibited generosity and joy. This is an astounding contrast. The average person gives once he has enough to support his chosen lifestyle. The Macedonians gave in the context of their lack of resources. Statistics show that those who make $10,000 or less tend to give away 5.5 percent of their income, while those who make $100,000 or more give only 2.9 percent. Generosity

---

2 Ibid., Romans 15:25–27.

is not hampered by a lack of resources, and it is not the sole preroga-
tive of the wealthy.

Their giving was sacrificial

In verse 3 of 2 Corinthians 8, it says that they gave "far more than
they could afford." Here we see the Macedonians making a difficult
situation even more difficult for themselves by giving more. Most of
us in this situation would limit our giving. Not the Macedonians!
John Piper challenges our notions of wealth and security in the following statement:

> The point is: a $70,000 salary does not have to be accompa-
> nied by a $70,000 lifestyle. God is calling us to be conduits
> of his grace, not cul-de-sacs. Our great danger today is
> thinking that the conduit should be lined with gold. It
> shouldn't. Copper will do. No matter how grateful we are,
> gold will not make the world think that our God is good;
> it will make people think that our God is gold. That is no
> honor to the supremacy of his worth.[3]

I had a friend who was audited by the IRS because they thought there
was something unusual about the amount he claimed he had given
away one year. How many of us raise the eyebrows of the IRS when
they look at what we give away?

Their giving was spontaneous

Verses 4–5 tell us that they were "pleading for the privilege of
helping out in the relief of poor Christians. This was totally spontaneous, entirely their own idea, and caught us completely off guard."
Can you believe that? Here is a poverty-stricken Gentile congregation,
pleading for the opportunity to give to their hurting Jewish brothers.
Notice who is doing the begging here: it is not Paul! Paul does not
have to coerce them or heap guilt on their consciences. Do you beg to
give away your resources? Are you working passionately to find ways
to bless others? This is a sign of true generosity.

---

3   John Piper, *Let the Nations Be Glad: The Supremacy of God in Missions* (Grand
Rapids: Baker Book House, 1993), 16.

Their giving was an act of submission

Were they submitting to Paul, the great apostle, or his visionary ministry? Neither; first they submitted to God, then to their brothers and sisters in Christ in Jerusalem. Verse 5 makes this clear. Their giving was caught up in their relationship to God and their solidarity with their spiritual family.

Their giving was a spiritual barometer

In verse 12 Paul says, "The heart regulates the hands." In other words, their behavior was an indication of what was going on in their souls. Their giving was proof of how much the grace of Christ was working in them. What does your checkbook say about the grace of Christ in your life? To what degree is your heart being transformed so that it expresses itself in generosity of this kind?

Comparison Two: The Giving of Jesus

Paul connects the radical generosity of the Macedonians to the rich gift they have received in Christ. Their generosity is only a dim reflection of the generosity of Jesus. Paul reminds them of this when he says, "You are familiar with the generosity of our Master, Jesus Christ. Rich as he was, he gave it all away for us—in one stroke he became poor and we became rich" (v. 9). The motivation that drove them was not a moral code and the guideline of the tithe. It was a desire to show their gratitude for the immense treasures that were theirs because of Jesus's willingness to give all he had to them.

Think about who you were before you became a Christian. You were poor, alienated from God, an object of his wrath, enslaved to sin, and condemned to eternal death. But in Christ, you are reconciled to God, an object of his affection, a recipient of his cleansing work on the cross, a temple of the Holy Spirit, and immensely rich! Placing your confidence in this reality is what will make you generous. Because you are the recipient of God's riches in Christ, you are willing to share with others not simply out of your abundance, but even when you have to sacrifice.

Look at your relationship to money. What does it tell you about your relationship to God? What does it reveal about what you think is most important? How much does your personal "kingdom" of pleasure, comfort, security, and status have a hold on you? To what degree is the kingdom of God driving your life? Our money is an intensely personal part of our lives, and only an intensely personal relationship with the Redeemer can loosen our grasp on other things.

Time and People

Apart from sleeping, how do you spend most of your time? Like money, time is a window into your soul. It reveals to what degree you are being transformed by the grace of Christ. Time is a resource we all have in equal quantities. What does your use of time say about your attitude toward God and others? In Ephesians 5:15–21, Paul says,

> Be very careful, then, how you live—not as unwise but as wise, making the most of every opportunity, because the days are evil. Therefore do not be foolish, but understand what the Lord's will is. Do not get drunk on wine, which leads to debauchery. Instead, be filled with the Spirit. Speak to one another with psalms, hymns and spiritual songs. Sing and make music in your heart to the Lord, always giving thanks to God the Father for everything, in the name of our Lord Jesus Christ.
>
> Submit to one another out of reverence for Christ.

Like his comments about money in Ephesians 4:28, Paul connects his comments about time to our relationships with other Christians and the world. He says, "Make the most of every opportunity, because the days are evil" (v. 16). The King James translation says, "Redeeming the time, because the days are evil." What does this mean?

The call to "redeem the time" is similar to *carpe diem*, the Latin phrase for "seize the day." A more literal translation of "redeem the time" would be "buy up the time." The Greek word for "time" used here is not *chronos*, which refers to the passing of time in hours, months, and years. Instead, *kairos* is used, which the Bible uses to refer to the time between Jesus's first and second comings. This is a time of unique opportunity for us to display the grace of Christ to others. One day this season will come to an end when Christ returns in power and glory.

Thus a more awkward but appropriate rendering of this verse would be, "As you go about your life in this 'in-between time,' use it to its fullest to display the grace of Christ to others." In light of this new information, how do we understand what this verse is asking of us?

It is not calling you to frenetic activity

This passage is not encouraging unwise activity that overloads your schedule with church events and obligations. Nor does it ask you to turn normal relational moments into abnormal witnessing encounters. In fact, this behavior may hinder you from living wisely. Using your time wisely may include formal ministry opportunities like a missions trip, teaching a Sunday school class, or working in the nursery; but the call here is not so much about specific activities as it is about a lifestyle committed to God's purposes, encompassing all the details of daily life.

It means that you see your life in light of your various callings

This passage is saying, "Make the most of every area in which God has placed you." Are you single, married, retired, parent, child, friend, employer, employee, student, or grandparent? These are all callings and seasons of life, and you are to see them as opportunities to display the grace of Christ. Our tendency is to live with a "get through this season" mentality. We say to ourselves, *If I can just get through this busy season of life, then I will be okay.* This is an ungodly understanding of your current responsibilities and opportunities. I have a tendency to do this with parenting: *If I can just get through the diaper phase. . . .* Once my children were out of diapers, it became: *If I can just get through these early years of elementary school, then I can minister to others.* But if I am not careful, I will wish my life away and miss many opportunities to love and serve my children. These are missed opportunities to die to self and grow in grace. God wants us to see the daily struggles of life as critical moments of redemptive opportunity, rather than hindrances.

It means that you are to seize the little moments of life

Did you know that ninety-five percent of your life is lived in the mundane? For example, suppose a husband and wife are upset with each other. Will they turn toward each other or will they remain angry? This is a mammoth redemptive moment—huge! Consider how many of these moments you miss every day. Imagine if this couple misses thousands of these over the course of their marriage. Where will their marriage be in twenty years? Imagine if, instead, they took advantage of these times. Can you see the difference this would make?

You must see the context in which these things take place

Paul says, "Because the days are evil." You live in a war zone. You get out of bed every morning and there is a battle raging for your soul, your life, your friendships, and your marriage. You can't afford to waste these moments. The war is won in the little skirmishes that take place throughout your life. "Wake up!" Paul says. "You are at war."

Money, Time, and People

Do you see how money and time reveal your heart in relation to God and others? How you use time and money in your human relationships says much about your relationship with God. Because God is committed to glorifying himself, he sent his Son to redeem his creation. And at the top of the list of what he intends to redeem are people. He lavishes his resources on us so that we might participate in his kingdom work and dwell with him forever when he brings it to completion.

Are your priorities in line with God's? Do you invest in the things he does? Do other people share in God's blessings to you, or do you hoard them all for yourself? We are called to love God and use his blessings to love others. But sadly, we often use other people to get the things we love.

When I got married, I did what every other groom does. I repeated vows to my wife that said I would love her sacrificially all the days of my life. Who was I kidding? I look back and see how little I understood what I promised. What I was really thinking, to a large degree, was, *This is great! I love me and now you are going to love me!* My love was very shallow. It only took a few days of marriage to figure that out! God had plans to use my wife and children to show me just how shallow my love was and to help it deepen as I saw how much I needed to grow. Seeing this caused me to depend on God and his grace all the more.

There is not a day that passes that I don't struggle with the way I use my time and money with my family. And these are people I say I love! I struggle to hold my time loosely when I don't want to be disturbed. I find myself flinching when one of my children asks me for a few dollars to go out with friends. These daily reminders reveal a heart still in need of a major overhaul. The only thing capable of penetrating the hardness of my heart is the gracious redemption that Father, Son, and Spirit have accomplished on my behalf. If my heart is going to be changed, it has to remain immersed in that grace.

Think about a steak. If you want it to be tender and flavorful, you will put it in a marinade for a while before you place it on the grill. If we are going to love others with our time and money, something similar needs to happen with our hearts. Our hearts are hard and full of gristle. The way to soften them is to let them soak in God's redemptive grace in Christ. This is the only thing powerful enough to loosen our grip on money and time and produce real change. The gospel reminds me that everything I have is from God. Romans 8:32 says, "He who did not spare his own Son, but gave him up for us all—how will he not also, along with him, graciously give us all things?" This is worth pondering. In fact, it is the only thing that will enable you to live out everything we have talked about so far.

14

Provision

How long must I wrestle with my thoughts
and every day have sorrow in my heart?

Psalm 13:2

Brian and Kara had been married for eight years. They were facing a mountain of problems. Both had grown up in privileged families and been given all that life had to offer. Both sets of parents had high expectations for their futures and had provided everything they believed essential for success. Brian, Kara, and their siblings had been expected to take advantage of all these opportunities and use them to attain excellence.

Brian and Kara responded to their upbringings very differently. Born much later than his siblings, Brian always lived in their shadow. His brother was a prominent surgeon in a teaching hospital, and his sister was a high-powered lawyer in a top firm. Brian felt as though all eyes were on him, wondering how he would match their achievements. In his third year of college, the cracks began to show. After several semesters of near-failing grades in his pre-law classes, he decided to study philosophy. This was deeply disappointing to his parents and they were quite vocal about it. They also orchestrated calls of "concern" from his brother and sister to reinforce the message. Brian's struggle with depression started at that time.

Kara, on the other hand, was the oldest of four children. She was the recipient of her parents' encouragement and never suffered the comparisons Brian did. Those years of encouragement gave her the confidence to believe she could do almost anything. She finished her undergraduate degree with honors and went on to graduate from law school at the top of her class.

When Brian and Kara met, it seemed like a perfect match. Kara was drawn to Brian's pensive, sensitive personality. He was her retreat from the pressures of performance. Brian was drawn to Kara because she was like his family in many ways; he knew his parents would approve. Their common childhood experiences made it easy for them to talk to each other. It was so easy, in fact, that it kept them from seeing that they were two very different people.

Brian's sensitivity and Kara's achievements at first functioned as the bond in their relationship, but they would later become the fault line at the center of their problems. Kara did not realize until after they were married that Brian had abandoned the achievement dream she cherished. She didn't know that their relationship would challenge everything that was important to her professionally, materially, socially, and personally. Brian didn't realize that Kara would expect the same things of him that his parents did. As their marriage went on, an unhealthy dynamic developed. Brian slid deeper into depression as he realized that he was not living up to Kara's expectations. Kara responded to Brian's apathy and depression by incessantly pushing and prodding him to accomplish something and by complaining when he failed to complete even menial tasks around the house. However, the more Kara tried to control Brian, the more he would withdraw. It was a vicious spiral that was taking them both down.

The fallout was evident on many levels. Brian was starting his sixth job as a part-time philosophy professor at the local community college. Kara had created an internet business that allowed her to stay at home with their two children. The income from these jobs didn't come close to the lavish lifestyles they had once known. They were embarrassed by their apartment; they wouldn't invite their families over because it only reminded them of their failure. Because Brian tended to avoid conflict and Kara tended to confront, their conversations got ugly fast, even on small matters. They couldn't agree on parenting decisions, so their relationships with their children suffered. Their friendships at their local church were suffering too. Though they tried to maintain a positive appearance, the tension between them made it increasingly awkward for others to be around them. Finally, in an act of desperation, Kara called for help. Brian had faded deeper into depression and she was at the end of her rope. She called a woman who had shared her own struggles at church. Kara thought she might understand what she was going through.

Life as Kara Sees It

The "reality" you see will be the reality you live by. That was certainly true for Kara. As her friend from church listened to Kara's litany of problems and disappointments, she knew that there was no quick fix. A big part of Kara's struggle was the fact that all she saw was problems. Nothing in her world seemed to be going right. She felt isolated and alone, with no one who understood. Being around other people who appeared to have it all together only fueled this false assumption.

Another Take on Kara's World

As Kara's friend listened, she was moved by her suffering. She could remember being in a similar situation several years before. It wasn't hard to empathize and she wisely did not minimize the problems in Kara's life. Yet as she looked into Kara's world, she saw things that Kara could not see. Everywhere she looked, she saw the evidence of God's redeeming grace at work. She saw Kara's love for her husband and children. Though their finances were tight, she saw God's obvious provision. Where Kara saw only failure, her friend saw God's ability to use the struggles to bring this couple to a new place in their lives and marriage. She saw a church ready to offer support and help. From what Kara said, it seemed clear that Brian was willing to ask for help as well.

The most obvious sign of God's presence was the least obvious to Kara: the conversation she was having at that moment. The very fact that Kara, who was so self-confident, was admitting that she needed help was a wonderful mark of God's grace in her life. But because of what she did not see, Kara was stuck. She was panicky and despairing because God was the last person she thought about. Kara lacked hope and encouragement because her perspective lacked the God who was already acting on her behalf and on behalf of Brian and their family.

Explanation: Is It Enough?

When we are in the midst of trying circumstances, our tendency is to search for an explanation that does three things:

Helps us understand what is going on

We want to understand our struggle. Kara wants to know why Brian acts the way he does. She wants to know why she feels toward him the way she does. How did Brian change from someone so appealing to someone so unpleasant? These are all very good questions.

Points us to where we should be going

When things are difficult, there comes a time when we give up on grander purposes and settle for survival. We stop asking, "What can be?" and ask instead, "Will I make it?" Kara wants some goals that will give her purpose and motivation. These too are good desires.

Tells us how to get there

After seeing what is going on and where we need to be, we want practical skills and an action plan to get there. Kara wants to know how to make progress in her difficulty. These good things should also not be minimized.

However, despite these positive elements, explanations alone will only increase Kara's despair over time. There may be some initial encouragement, but it will not last. This is because explanations alone will convince Kara that the problems are deeper than she thought, the goals farther away, and her practical skills inadequate for the difficulty. Kara and Brian don't need something less than explanation: they need something *more*.

Imagination: The Rest of the Story

Kara's understanding of her situation is distorted by what she does not see. Let's say that someone has a ten thousand dollar debt, but does not know that an inheritance of one hundred thousand dollars is coming. Won't that affect the way the person looks at the debt? Kara and Brian see their set of ten thousand dollar problems, but they do not see the billion dollar provision God has made available to them. What they lack is not explanation, but imagination.

Imagination is not the ability to dream up things that aren't real; it is the ability to see what is real but often unseen. As Eugene Peterson says in *Subversive Spirituality*, for a Christian whose hope is in an invisible God, seeing the unseen is essential.[1] Hebrews 11 calls this faith. Let Peterson stretch your thinking as he describes faith in terms of *imagination*.

> When I look at a tree, most of what I "see" I do not see at all. I see a root system beneath the surface, sending tendrils through the soil sucking up nutrients out of the loam. I see the light pouring energy into the leaves. I see the fruit that will appear in a few months. I stare and stare and see the bare branches austere in next winter's snow and wind. I see all that, I really do—I am not making it up. But I could not photograph it. I see it by means of imagination. If my imagination is stunted or inactive, I will only see what I can use, or something that is in my way.[2]

What Peterson is saying is profound but not new. He is describing something we do all the time. Whenever parents help their child with homework, they imagine the child's future high school and college years. When a couple sits down to discuss finances, they anticipate their future retirement. Parents saving for a special vacation encourage their children to imagine what it will be like; it takes the sting out of the sacrifices needed to afford it. When the children complain, the parents remind them of the fun times ahead. The children learn to live with hardship because they are learning to see the unseen.

Imagination gives us a deeper sense of two unseen realities: (1) our identity, the unseen realities of who God says we are; and (2) God's resources, the unseen realities of his presence with us and provision for us.

Identity: Who Am I?

Imagine standing in an art gallery where the walls are covered with beautiful paintings. The only problem is that the lights are out and

---

1   Eugene Peterson, *Subversive Spirituality* (Grand Rapids: Eerdmans, 1997), 160.
2   Ibid., 161.

you can't see them! Imagine that wonderful music is playing, but your ears are plugged with cotton. Imagine that you are eating an exquisite meal, but a head cold causes the flavors to run over your tongue unnoticed. This is true of Kara spiritually. She cannot see and experience the things that are true because she lacks spiritual sight, hearing, and taste. Her perspective is dominated by what is wrong in her life and relationships. They are the realities she lives by. Imagination, or faith, does not mean that Kara should deny her present circumstances; it does mean, however, that she should see them in the context of the whole picture, which includes who she is in Christ.

We often miss the unseen things that are true of us as God's children. But the Bible says that two fundamental things characterize those who are in Christ. First, there has been a radical change in the core of our being. The Bible says that our hearts of stone have been replaced by hearts of flesh. Ezekiel 36:26 says, "I will give you a new heart and put a new spirit in you; I will remove from you your heart of stone and give you a heart of flesh." Paul is referring to the same thing when he says we are a new creation in Christ (2 Corinthians 5:17). This wonderful reality does not mean that we have become perfect, but that our hearts are malleable, sensitive, and alive to God.

For Kara and Brian, this amazing truth means that they are not stuck even though they are obviously struggling in their marriage. But they need imagination (that is, faith) to see their true potential for change. We often get stuck when repeatedly confronted with problems, failure, weakness, disappointment, and sin. Our track record tends to convince us that change is impossible. Imagination does not deny the track record, but places it in the context of who we are in Christ. It reminds us that God's Spirit is at work in us and we are "partakers of the divine nature" (2 Peter 1:4, NASB). Thus Brian and Kara have been gifted by God with the potential for change.

The Bible also stirs our imagination by explaining our connection to God as his children. Our new standing is legal, but it is also personal and practical. Marriage and adoption both involve legal unions, but ones that are intended to create relationships that are far more than legal contracts. Imagine a married couple who only related at a legal level without love. Their marriage would be no different than a business partnership. What if adoptive parents only related to their new child in terms of their legal obligations to feed, clothe, and educate him? The words "I love you" would never be uttered. This would be horrific because the new legal status is intended to be the context in which a deeper, fuller relationship flourishes. Marital and parent-child relationships are not less than legal; they are much more!

In the same way, our reconciliation with God gives us a relationship with him that should alter the way we respond to everything. God is now my Father and I am his child. He looks on me with favor. I am the object of his attention and affection. I have access to his care. He blesses me with his resources. He offers ongoing forgiveness and cleansing as I struggle with sin. He promises never to leave or forsake me. He makes a commitment to finish the work of change he has begun in me.

Brian and Kara attend a good church where their new legal standing with God has been taught, but their personal understanding has remained theoretical. They have never learned how to connect it to their everyday experience so, while it sounds good on Sunday morning, it has no relevance on Tuesday evening when they are in the middle of a fight. They have no real idea what their new relationship with Christ is really about. Jesus's personal presence with Brian and Kara in the midst of conflict is never acknowledged. They don't stop to ask him for help because they don't think of him as a person. They think of him more in terms of a lawyer who has managed to keep them from going to jail. Now that they are past that danger, they don't keep on relating to him.

What are the implications of these things for Brian, Kara, and for us? It means that each of us can have hope when we get out of bed in the morning; we know that the Lord of heaven and earth is truly our Father. This is what it means to live by faith. Imagination takes us to the mountaintop of God's grace so we can see our struggles and challenges from the vantage point of his relentless love for us.

Imagine Kara connecting with Christ personally each morning and talking to him like this: "Jesus, thank you for being with me right now and through this day. Because of you, I am never alone. Because of you, I don't have to manage the universe—or even Brian! Please give me your strength to entrust Brian to you; help me to love him in ways that will help both of us to see you and to love you and each other." Imagine Brian uttering words like, "Father, I know I have looked to things like status and success for a sense of well-being. I've grown depressed when

I couldn't achieve them. I have minimized your immense love for me in Christ. For that, I deserve your condemnation. But because of what Christ has done for me, I am accepted by you—not just tolerated, but wonderfully embraced by you. As I take each step today, help me to know that you are for me and with me. While I may struggle with depression, I am first and foremost your beloved child. Let these truths and your personal presence give me courage to move into my life and my relationship with Kara." In these little vignettes, Brian and Kara are putting faith into action. They are communing with the unseen God because their imagination is enabling them to see reality. As Kara's friend steered them to people in the church who could help them, this is what Kara and Brian began to learn how to do.

God's Presence and Provision

What else do Brian and Kara need to see with the eyes of faith imagination? When struggles remain and life does not change overnight, it is easy for confusion and helplessness to settle in. These things cloud the imagination. They lead you to think that the struggles of your life are unique, that no one understands, and that you are all alone. Trying harder only seems to aggravate the problem. You try your best to figure it out, but you still don't come up with any answers.

When you are in this place of neediness and discouragement, you want answers and strategies, but God gives us something better. God's provision simply can't be reduced to answers and strategies because his provision is tied to his presence. God knows that our need is much bigger and deeper than what we think will satisfy it. So he not only gives us practical advice, he gives us himself. *He* is our wisdom. *He* is our strength. *He* is our forgiveness. *He* is our Father. As Moses said in Exodus 33:15, "If your Presence does not go with us, do not send us up from here." Moses knew that if God is not near, all the strategies and techniques in the world won't help against overwhelming odds. Jesus takes this reality of presence and provision a step further in John 14. He says that he will not just be near us or with us, but *in* us.

If you love me, you will obey what I command. And I will ask the Father, and he will give you another Counselor to be with you forever—the Spirit of truth. The world cannot accept him, because it neither sees him nor knows him. But you know him, for he lives with you and will be in you. I will not leave you as orphans; I will come to you. Before long, the world will not see me anymore, but you will see me. Because I live, you also will live. On that day you will realize that I am in my Father, and you are in me, and I am in you. (John 14:15–20)

Jesus describes his presence in terms of a family relationship when he says he will not leave us as orphans. Brian and Kara need to face their struggles with the knowledge that God, the ultimate source of all they need, is living inside them. In the midst of their difficulty, Brian and Kara do not have to despair and feel alone in their struggles; God is present. They don't have to resort to speaking words that hurt; they can speak words that heal. They don't have to succumb to disappointment, bitterness, and vengeance; they can choose to be patient, kind, forgiving, and compassionate. They can encourage rather than condemn. They can bear each other's burdens and serve each other with joy. The promises of new potential don't have to be seen through jaded eyes; they can be received in a way that fosters new, heartfelt hope and obedience, even if things don't get better right away. Why? Because their imagination now sees not simply a restored marriage, but a deeper, moment-by-moment personal relationship with God. Ultimately, this is why Brian and Kara have been created and redeemed.

The stakes are high: the reality our imagination embraces is the reality we will live by. If we are not captured by the truth of living in a deeply personal relationship with God, we will shrink our expectations and dreams down to the size of our own selfish wants, desires, and strategies. This is what has happened to Brian and Kara, and it often happens to the rest of us. Brian was being crushed by the pressure to attain success as others had defined it. Now he was seeing that God was making him into something far more glorious: God was making him like Christ. Kara had allowed her vision for life to shrink to the size of controlling her little corner of the universe. But now she was seeing for the first time that God was already in control. She could trust him to change Brian because she was beginning to trust him to change her.

What Is God Doing in My Life?

When we don't see our identity in Christ or his presence and provision for us, we wind up envisioning a God too busy to care about us. Prayer becomes little more than a spiritual 911 call. To get God's attention, we "make the call" so that God will wake up, see our needs, act on our behalf, and provide rescue. But once he shows up and does what we think he should, we assume that he then retreats to take care of other pressing matters until we call again.

This flies in the face of the reality of who God is and how he works, but it is how Brian and Kara have tended to view him. To them, he was distant and inactive. In fact, Kara had wondered aloud why God had not done something to help her marriage. Brian wondered why God did not lift his depression. Their view of God's passivity was a principal ingredient in their abiding hopelessness. So was their focus on circumstances, which kept them from seeing their deeper heart issues of success, control, and acceptance that needed to be addressed by the power of the gospel.

Once again, the Scriptures enlarge our imagination by helping us see things we don't normally see. The Scriptures increase our awareness of a God who is near, willing, and able to save. In Psalm 121, the psalmist points to God's abiding presence and tireless activity on our behalf:

> I lift up my eyes to the hills—
>   where does my help come from?
> My help comes from the LORD,
>   the Maker of heaven and earth.
> He will not let your foot slip—
>   he who watches over you will not slumber;
> indeed, he who watches over Israel
>   will neither slumber nor sleep.
> The LORD watches over you—
>   the LORD is your shade at your right hand;
> the sun will not harm you by day,
>   nor the moon by night.
> The LORD will keep you from all harm—
>   he will watch over your life;
> the LORD will watch over your coming and going
>   both now and forevermore.

The same picture of God is seen in the life and words of the apostle Paul. In the midst of many struggles and pressures, Paul says in Romans 8:28–39,

> And we know that in all things God works for the good of those who love him, who have been called according to his purpose. For those God foreknew he also predestined to be conformed to the likeness of his Son, that he might be the firstborn among many brothers. And those he predestined, he also called; those he called, he also justified; those he justified, he also glorified.
>
> What, then, shall we say in response to this? If God is for us, who can be against us? He who did not spare his own Son, but gave him up for us all—how will he not also, along with him, graciously give us all things? Who will bring any charge against those whom God has chosen? It is God who justifies. Who is he that condemns? Christ Jesus, who died—more than that, who was raised to life—is at the right hand of God and is also interceding for us. Who shall separate us from the love of Christ? Shall trouble or hardship or persecution or famine or nakedness or danger or sword? As it is written:
>
> "For your sake we face death all day long;
>   we are considered as sheep to be slaughtered."
>
> No, in all these things we are more than conquerors through him who loved us. For I am convinced that neither death nor life, neither angels nor demons, neither the present nor the future, nor any powers, neither height nor depth, nor anything else in all creation, will be able to separate us from the love of God that is in Christ Jesus our Lord.

How radically these verses confront our feeble imaginations! When we are in trouble, our tendency is to think that God is nowhere to be found and we must fix things ourselves. When our vision of reality is this small, our attempts to fix things often make the trouble more troubling. We either want to fix the wrong things or fix the right things in the wrong way.

The Bible not only tells us that God works continuously, it also tells us how he works and what he is working on. This gives us hope and gives our work purpose and direction. When we start working off the same script as God, we function in ways that are truly redemptive. If God forgives, we must work to forgive. If he is working to make someone a better person, we should do what we can to encourage those changes. If God is working to make peace, we are to be peacemakers. If God daily bears our burdens, we want to help shoulder the burdens of others. If God is working to produce hearts of worship in us, we should seek to stimulate adoration in one another. In short, we are called to help each other see the unseen reality of our active, present, and personal God. God's work is driven by an agenda so much grander than simply making our lives better. He wants to remake us into his likeness. And that likeness can be seen in Jesus.

Many explanations could be offered to Brian and Kara about why things have gone wrong and how they can try to fix them. But explanations alone will not bring them to a new place in their marriage. Explanation by itself may bring temporary insight and change, but nothing that lasts. The vastness of God's glory needs to loom so large before their eyes that they can see their problems in proper perspective. The courage to hope for lasting change is only as big as the God their imagination—and ours—is able to see. When I see my identity in Christ, God's presence and provision, and what he is doing in the process, I am willing and able to do things I wouldn't do otherwise. Brian and Kara are beginning to do this in small but important ways.

Explanation, while an important aspect of change, is not sufficient. It must be fueled by imagination. Eugene Peterson captures the vital interplay between the two.

> We have a pair of mental operations, imagination and explanation, designed to work in tandem. When the gospel is given robust and healthy expression, the two work in graceful synchronicity. Explanation pins things down so that we can handle and use them—obey and teach, help and guide. Imagination opens things up so that we can grow into maturity—worship and adore, exclaim and honor, follow and trust. Explanation restricts and defines and holds down; imagination expands and lets loose. Explanation keeps our

feet on the ground; imagination lifts our heads into the clouds. Explanation puts us in harness; imagination catapults us into mystery. Explanation reduces life to what can be used; imagination enlarges life into what can be adored.[3]

Living in God's Big Sky Country

As you have been reading, maybe you've been thinking, *Okay, Paul and Tim, this sounds good, but how do I stimulate my imagination?* How do you stimulate your imagination in any area of life? If you have a vision for decorating your house, you buy decorating magazines and pore over them until you get an idea of what you want to do. If you want to take a vacation, you sit down with someone who has been where you want to go. You talk about his trip, gaining insight and excitement about what you can do when you get there. You will probably get travel brochures or look at the pictures from your friend's trip.

It is not enough for Brian and Kara to work on their marriage; they need to work on their imaginations. God has given them ways to do that. He has provided simple means that stimulate and enlarge their imaginations to see what they need to see. These means are prayer, truth, fellowship, worship, and the sacraments. We are tempted to minimize those means because they seem so ordinary. And when we approach them without a clear sense of why they were given, we can miss the profound impact they should have on us.

Bible study and personal reading fall flat when we miss what Bible study and reading are meant to do. They are intended to be a means, not an end. The purpose of Bible study is to give me a vision of the God who is my Savior and with whom I am in relationship. Bible study is intended to stimulate worship, but so often it is focused on theology and rules. My relationships with my brothers and sisters in the body of Christ are intended to stimulate our collective appreciation of God's greatness and grace. But so often relationships become an end in themselves, serving our desires for acceptance. The Lord's Supper is a rich experience where spiritual truths are laid before us in tangible ways. It is intended to stir our imaginations to see the grace of God through taste, touch, and sight. But many times the Lord's Supper becomes nothing more than a ritual we perform by rote.

3   Ibid., 167.

There are many other things God provides to stir up our faith imagination: hymns and songs, sermons, seminars, poetry, allegory, physical creation, and short-term mission trips, to name a few. The natural world should stimulate our imagination. The life and ministry of the body of Christ should expand our faith and worship. In the midst of life's struggles and opportunities, we all need to ask how our imaginations can be stimulated to see and worship God. We should also look for the means God has given us to make this happen.

The reality your imagination sees is the reality that will shape your words, actions, attitudes, and relationships. The question is not, "Has God made adequate provision?" The question is, "Do we see him? Are we responding to each other not just on the basis of personal strength, the size of the problem, or our track record, but on the basis of what God has provided?"

Brian and Kara look a lot like us. Like them, we forget that it is in the little moments that spiritual battles are lost and won. We tend to minimize the significance of the daily, moment-by-moment skirmishes with outward circumstances and inward sin. But Brian and Kara are beginning to see what it is like to depend on Christ in those little moments. Brian may still struggle with depression, but Christ is present with him, helping Brian to see himself through new eyes. Kara is on a similar journey. She is relinquishing her need to be in control and trusting God to make all things new—even her! While much change is still needed, the eyes of their hearts are being opened to see how wide, deep, broad, and long the love and glory of Christ are. As they see through eyes of faith (or the eyes of reality), Christ is changing them from one degree of glory to another. This is truly amazing, yet it is exactly what God has said is reality all along.

How are you viewing reality? Are you growing in your ability to see the unseen? The apostle Paul encourages and commands us to do this in Ephesians 5:14:

"Wake up, O sleeper,
    rise from the dead,
and Christ will shine on you."

15

Moving Out

*Do everything without complaining or arguing, so that you
may become blameless and pure, children of God without
fault in a crooked and depraved generation, in which you shine
like stars in the universe as you hold out the word of life. . . .*

Philippians 2:14–16

If you are a parent, ask your children how many of their friends
come from broken homes. If you are single, consider how many of
your relationships include some degree of pain and disappointment.
Take a look at your own family and extended family. We all live with,
and are party to, the damage sin engenders.

What makes the Bible so compelling is that it understands this.
The drama of Scripture is our drama. It rings true to life no matter
what degree of brokenness we have experienced. All of our lives are
riddled with moments of regret. Times when we want to take back
words we have spoken. Times when we want to turn back the clock
and undo a decision. Times when passion got in the way of principle.
We are learning as we go, and we get it right one minute and terri-
bly wrong the next. Motives collide with motives until it is hard to
figure out what is right. Sometimes you are fiercely irritated with a
person you deeply love. Sometimes you replay scenes over and over
in your head, even though you know you shouldn't. Sometimes every
moment of peace seems to be ruptured by conflict. And sometimes
there is much to be thankful for, but also much to mourn.

In light of all this, it is amazing that we still can find moments when things go right! The really stunning thing about our world is not the overwhelming amount of brokenness, but the presence of any good! The fact that relationships remain intact at all, and even last for years, is a sign that God's goodness still abides in the world.

Hope in the Ruins

Because of God's presence, you have experienced joy in relationships. Conflicts actually get resolved. A tough conversation turns out positively. Someone has reached out to you in a time of struggle. You have been granted forgiveness. Real love has been expressed and shared. You have been served and have been willing to serve. A casual relationship has matured into a deep friendship. People have overlooked your weaknesses and applauded your strengths. People have learned to be honest without being mean.

The Psalms express the brokenness and fragility of life in the cries of people who long for something that is truly better. And yet there is praise throughout the Psalms of Scripture too. It is not vacuous emotionalism, but rather praise that lives in the middle of fear, pain, hurt, and disappointment. The praise never ignores these experiences. Instead, it grows more thankful as it recognizes the redeeming God who meets us in life's pains and joys. A psalm that captures the meeting place of brokenness and grace is Psalm 57:1–2. Hear how the psalmist lives in this intersection as he faces the realities of life.

> Have mercy on me, O God, have mercy on me,
>   for in you my soul takes refuge.
> I will take refuge in the shadow of your wings
>   until the disaster has passed.
> I cry out to God Most High,
>   to God, who fulfills his purpose for me.

The psalmist does not flinch at life's hardships, but he does not gloss over them either. He acknowledges the reality of disaster and yet cries out to God in the midst of it. His psalm is one of pain-stained worship.

Life at the Intersection

Ben and Erin met when they were teenagers. Their friendship quickly became romantic because they felt like they had stumbled on a kind of love they never received at home. They found refuge in each other. Within a few months Erin was pregnant, and they faced the first of many difficult decisions. The embarrassment of the pregnancy led them to get married secretly, but they had little understanding of how to live together, and they didn't have a clue about how to love each other.

Ben was a boy in a man's body. He seemed more interested in the latest video game than the responsibilities of a husband and a father. He was a latchkey kid who had never been accountable to others. Erin's parents were divorced. They tried to make up for it by giving her gifts and indulging her every whim. She had been pampered in all the wrong ways and expected this kind of treatment as an expression of love. Ben did not have the desire or the resources to meet those expectations. Although he had made significant efforts to win her affection while they were dating, this changed as soon as they were married.

Erin's disappointment and Ben's feelings of failure, coupled with their inability to resolve conflict, turned the marriage into a war zone. Erin complained that Ben did not really love her; Ben complained that Erin was too demanding. They alternated between heated argument and cool withdrawal. In either case, they always pointed the finger at the other.

One evening their conflict spilled out into the stairwell of their apartment complex. Another couple overheard the argument and asked if they could help. As a result of this simple act of kindness, Erin began to meet with the wife and Ben started a friendship with the husband. They also spent time together as couples. These new friends were part of a local church that excelled in welcoming struggling people and discipling them in grace. Ben and Erin immediately found other couples who would honestly share about their struggles, which turned out to be surprisingly similar to their own. As people shared, what caught Ben and Erin's attention was the honesty that was tied to a strong hope for change. Significant personal changes began to take place in Ben and Erin as they came to trust in Christ. This simple yet powerful experience of the benefits of the gospel began to transform their marriage. They still had plenty of difficulty, but they began to deal with it differently. They were also surrounded by believers who were committed to reach out to them and persevere with them through the messy process of change now underway.

The Real Story

What began as a story about Ben and Erin is really a story about an unnamed couple and the quietly revolutionary community of faith to which they belong. The weapons of their warfare were humility, honesty, hope, grace, and courage. They moved toward Ben and Erin and invited them into their world.

What this couple did can be summarized by one word from the Bible: kingdom. The revolution of the kingdom of God is not noisy and explosive. It's a quiet revolution carried out by humble servants who often go unnoticed. Just consider the King of this radical new kingdom. How did Jesus enter human history? He came as a baby born into poverty amidst an oppressed people. He preached a message of hope that advanced through the quiet but powerful display of God's love through his suffering, death, and resurrection. Wherever this King is present, these same surprising virtues will be present. These were the qualities that won Ben and Erin's hearts.

What was it that drew Ben and Erin to this anonymous couple? Ben and Erin were fearful, hopeless, and desperate, but this anonymous couple was compelling. Their lives spoke of the power, hope, and reality of King Jesus. Ben and Erin felt as if they could trust them with their troubles. They, in turn, were willing to have their lives disrupted by needy people like Ben and Erin. Whenever God's grace changes your heart and life, you are experiencing the kingdom coming to earth as it already is in heaven. And when you experience this kingdom power in your life, you want others to experience it too.

Not What You're Looking For

In a conversation with the Pharisees, Jesus confronted their fundamental misunderstanding of the kingdom of God. They imagined a system of political rule in which they would be the ruling class. Jesus informs them that his kingdom is not a system, but the tangible display of the presence of the King.

> Once, having been asked by the Pharisees when the kingdom of God would come, Jesus replied, "The kingdom of God does not come with your careful observation, nor will people say, 'Here it is,' or 'There it is,' because the kingdom of God is within you." (Luke 17:20–21)

Because the Pharisees were looking for an earthly, political kingdom, they were looking to the future for its arrival. They were confused about what the visible display of the kingdom would be like. Many people have concluded from this passage that the kingdom is not visible, but that it resides in the hearts of people. The NIV reinforces this view by translating the last phrase to read "the kingdom of God is within you." But Jesus is saying, "The kingdom is in your midst," pointing to an internal and external reality.

Jesus is telling the Pharisees that the kingdom is right there for them to see, but they do not see it. He is saying that because the King is here, there are visible signs of his rule. What are these signs that go against what the Pharisees expect? Jesus is pointing to an internal reality of grace that expresses itself in observable changes in individuals and their relationships. It leaves a trail of humility, compassion, sacrifice, joy, and patience, along with many other qualities. The impact of this revolution will extend to systems and institutions, but this is not where it begins. It begins in the hearts of people and has ripple effects that spread to the farthest reaches of sin. Jesus is saying that the Pharisees are looking at the very King of the kingdom while wondering when the promised kingdom is going to come!

The Visible Invisible Kingdom

What does the kingdom of God have to do with Ben and Erin's story, or you and your relationships? Everything! If you are experiencing humility, forgiveness, patience, or godly conflict, you are experiencing the work of the King as he builds his kingdom. This means that your relationships are a place where the kingdom has come, and they are intended to attract others to the King. In addition, whenever you speak of change in your life and relationships, you are not drawing attention to your wisdom, relational savvy, or personal giftedness; you are calling attention to Jesus, your King. As the couple and community that reached out to Ben and Erin understood, the kingdom of God is not just for private enjoyment, but also for public display. People who come into our midst will see the work of the kingdom but they won't necessarily see the King. It is our responsibility and privilege to point them to him.

Making the Kingdom Visible

The Bible talks about the kingdom of God in many ways, but Jesus uses two metaphors to talk specifically about its visible nature. In Matthew 5:13–16, Jesus says that his kingly presence within his people enables them to function as salt and light to those around them.

> "You are the salt of the earth. But if the salt loses its saltiness, how can it be made salty again? It is no longer good for anything, except to be thrown out and trampled by men.
>
> "You are the light of the world. A city on a hill cannot be hidden. Neither do people light a lamp and put it under a bowl. Instead they put it on its stand, and it gives light to everyone in the house. In the same way, let your light shine before men, that they may see your good deeds and praise your Father in heaven."

Let's consider what this means for us and the redemptive opportunities all around us.

Being Salt: Moving Out

The image of salt challenges isolationism because salt is only effective as a retardant to decay when it is in close contact with the decaying substance. This is an uncomfortable call because it pulls us away from the comfort of relationships already transformed by the King. Yet we are most true to our identity and calling when we live in the midst of broken people. The call of the kingdom is a call into the world, never away from it. Jesus was unequivocal when he said in John 17:15, "My prayer is not that you take them out of the world but that you protect them from the evil one." We are to be in the world, though not of it. Often Christians have evaded the challenge of this call by defining their role as salt in negative terms. They have simply denounced bad things in the culture and been against things rather than for them.

But the image of salt also highlights the importance of our character. Salt is only effective if it is truly salty! We are called to be people of great character so that, when we come in contact with the world, our character influences those around us. These qualities are not just about courage and conviction, but humility and compassion as well. What we say is important, but how we say it is too. What you stand for is important, but who you are as you stand for those things is important too. If, by God's grace, you are truly "salty," God intends you to apply that salt to decayed relationships where it is most needed.

What ministry opportunities exist for you with the people God has put in your path?

- Is there a struggling family in your neighborhood?
- Is there a single parent at your child's school?
- Is there someone in your church who is lonely and discouraged?
- Is there a teenager who needs to see how a family functions?
- Are there relationships you can pursue through your children's extracurricular activities?
- Where are the needs for service, mercy, and help in your community?
- Has God put an elderly person in your life who needs companionship?
- Where are the poor in your community? How can you be a part of their lives?

These are some of the ways God may be moving you outward. You are not necessarily called to do all of these things because of other callings and responsibilities you already have. But God has undoubtedly given you opportunities to be salt. If you have children, you are called to care for them, but one way to care for them is to include them in some ministry opportunities God has given you.

One thing is certain: in order to be salt, you must be confident in the God who entered a sinful world to redeem it. Though we are to be wise, we are not to fear the world in which God has placed us. Yes, things will get messy. But if you are humbled by the messiness of sin in your own life, yet confident in God's grace to change you, you will not be afraid to get close to other sinners who need that same grace. God will use the messiness you encounter in others to spur your own growth in the gospel.

Being Light: Welcoming In

The good things we experience are a mark of God's kingdom coming to our own lives. If being salt involves stepping out into the world, being light involves welcoming people in so that they can see that the kingdom has come. You welcome people in so that they can see the impact of the kingdom on your relationships. Our relationships are meant to be beacons in a dark world, and we are called to welcome people into the light. The apostle Paul talked about the Christian community functioning as light in Philippians 2:14–16.

> Do everything without complaining or arguing, so that you may become blameless and pure, children of God without fault in a crooked and depraved generation, in which you shine like stars in the universe as you hold out the word of life. . . .

In Ephesians 5:11, Paul calls us to "expose" the "deeds of darkness." The word Paul uses for "exposing" the darkness does not mean "point a finger and judge." It means that we persuade people that the gospel is true because our lives are a compelling testimony to the God who has come for sinners. Paul continues his thought in verse 15, saying, "Be very careful, then, how you live—not as unwise but as wise, making the most of every opportunity, because the days are evil." Our lives and relationships in Christ are to be more compelling than the temporary pleasures of sin.

Keep in mind that one of the most compelling things people see is your own need for grace. This is not a ministry that benefits from an "I've arrived but you need grace" posture. It's in the context of your own sins, struggles, and weaknesses that the love and power of the King are most clearly seen. Both of us have had people live in our homes for extended periods of time. Invariably, our guests have said that the most helpful thing about the experience (in addition to the good things they observed) was the fact that they saw our sins and our daily need for grace. One mark of the kingdom is a humble awareness of the ongoing pull of sin, and the daily cries for help that result.

What opportunities do you have to invite others into the light so that they can see the kingdom?

- Does your child have a friend who may benefit from time in your home?
- Is there a coworker you can invite for dinner and a movie with your friends?
- Do you know an elderly person who would enjoy the love of a family during the holidays?
- Is there someone who is burdened or in crisis and in need of a retreat?
- Is there another family who would enjoy time with your family?
- Do you know a younger couple who could be mentored by an older couple?
- If you are single, is there a family with young children who would benefit from your help? How might this bless you as well?

Of course, you are not called to do all these things all the time. But be thinking of ways you can invite people into your life and start pursuing those opportunities in practical ways.

Unsung Heroes

The story of Ben and Erin was actually about the unnamed couple and their church community. For all of the weaknesses and failures this anonymous couple surely experienced, they got something very right about their relationship. They knew that the good things God had done for them were not meant to be kept for themselves; they were instruments God intended to use. This is how God's economy works. He lavishes sinners with grace and blessing so that they can do the same for others in his name.

Ministry Is Worship

The call we have considered in this chapter is not just a call to ministry; it is a call to worship. That might sound strange, but whenever you serve other people, you are not just serving them. You are serving the King—and that is worship. Love for Christ will always extend itself to others. Thankfulness to Christ will always result in sharing our blessings with others. Enjoying the benefits of Christ's forgiveness will always express itself in forgiveness to others. Gratitude for God's loving pursuit will always lead us to pursue others—even when they don't want to be pursued. Thankfulness for Christ's willingness to enter our messy world will make us willing to enter someone else's. Worship recognizes that our good relationships do not belong to us, but to Christ. Therefore, we cannot hoard them; we are compelled to share them with others. Our responses to people are always connected to our response to Christ. Our worship and theology will always be on display in the way we treat others. Christ closed the gap between our vertical and horizontal relationships with these startling and humbling words in Matthew 25:34–40:

> "Then the King will say to those on his right, 'Come, you who are blessed by my Father; take your inheritance, the kingdom prepared for you since the creation of the world. For I was hungry and you gave me something to eat, I was thirsty and you gave me something to drink, I was a stranger and you invited me in, I needed clothes and you clothed me, I was sick and you looked after me, I was in prison and you came to visit me.'
>
> "Then the righteous will answer him, 'Lord, when did we see you hungry and feed you, or thirsty and give you something to drink? When did we see you a stranger and invite you in, or needing clothes and clothe you? When did we see you sick or in prison and go to visit you?'
>
> "The King will reply, 'I tell you the truth, whatever you did for one of the least of these brothers of mine, you did for me.'"

Aren't you glad that this is exactly what Jesus did for you?